Extreme Programming
for Web Projects

The XP Series

Kent Beck, Series Advisor

Extreme Programming, familiarly known as XP, is a discipline of business and software development that focuses both parties on common, reachable goals. XP teams produce quality software at a sustainable pace. The practices that make up "book" XP are chosen for their dependence on human creativity and acceptance of human frailty.

Although XP is often presented as a list of practices, XP is not a finish line. You don't get better and better grades at doing XP until you finally receive the coveted gold star. XP is a starting line. It asks the question, "How little can we do and still build great software?"

The beginning of the answer is that, if we want to leave software development uncluttered, we must be prepared to completely embrace the few practices we adopt. Half measures leave problems unsolved to be addressed by further half measures. Eventually you are surrounded by so many half measures that you can no longer see that the heart of the value programmers create comes from programming.

I say, "The beginning of the answer …" because there is no final answer. The authors in the XP Series have been that and done there, and returned to tell their story. The books in this series are the signposts they have planted along the way: "Here lie dragons," "Scenic drive next 15 km," "Slippery when wet."

Excuse me, I gotta go program.

Titles in the Series

Extreme Programming Applied: Playing to Win, Ken Auer and Roy Miller

Extreme Programming Examined, Giancarlo Succi and Michele Marchesi

Extreme Programming Explained: Embrace Change, Kent Beck

Extreme Programming Explored, William C. Wake

Extreme Programming for Web Projects, Doug Wallace, Isobel Raggett, and Joel Aufgang

Extreme Programming in Practice, James W. Newkirk and Robert C. Martin

Extreme Programming Installed, Ron Jeffries, Ann Anderson, and Chet Hendrickson

Extreme Programming Perspectives, Michele Marchesi, Giancarlo Succi, Don Wells, and Laurie Williams

Planning Extreme Programming, Kent Beck and Martin Fowler

Questioning Extreme Programming, Pete McBreen

Testing Extreme Programming, Lisa Crispin and Tip House

For more information, check out the series Web site at http://www.awprofessional.com/series/XP/

Extreme Programming
for Web Projects

Doug Wallace

Isobel Raggett

Joel Aufgang

✦Addison-Wesley

Boston • San Francisco • New York • Toronto • Montreal
London • Munich • Paris • Madrid
Capetown • Sydney • Tokyo • Singapore • Mexico City

Many of the designations used by manufacturers and sellers to distinguish their products are claimed as trademarks. Where those designations appear in this book, and Addison-Wesley was aware of a trademark claim, the designations have been printed with initial capital letters or in all capitals.

The authors and publisher have taken care in the preparation of this book, but make no expressed or implied warranty of any kind and assume no responsibility for errors or omissions. No liability is assumed for incidental or consequential damages in connection with or arising out of the use of the information or programs contained herein.

The publisher offers discounts on this book when ordered in quantity for bulk purchases and special sales. For more information, please contact:

U.S. Corporate and Government Sales
(800) 382-3419
corpsales@pearsontechgroup.com

For sales outside of the U.S., please contact:

International Sales
(317) 581-3793
international@pearsontechgroup.com

Visit Addison-Wesley on the Web: *www.awprofessional.com*

Library of Congress Cataloging-in-Publication Data
Wallace, Doug
    Extreme programming for Web projects / Doug Wallace, Isobel Raggett, Joel Aufgang
        p.   cm.
    Includes bibliographical references and index.
    ISBN 0-201-79427-6 (alk. paper)
        1. Computer software—Development. 2. eXtreme programming. 3. Web site
    development.   I. Raggett, Isobel. II. Aufgang, Joel. III. Title.

    QA76.76.D47 W348 2003
    005.1'1--dc21

                                                            2002027668

    Pearson Education, Inc.
    Rights and Contracts Department
    75 Arlington Street, Suite 300
    Boston, MA 02116
    Fax: (617) 848-7047

ISBN 0-201-79427-6
Text printed on recycled paper
1 2 3 4 5 6 7 8 9 10—MA—0605040302
First printing, September 2002

To my sister Tracy

—Doug

To my loving parents
and my sister Charlotte

—Isobel

To my Darling Rosemary

—Joel

Contents

Web development is an adolescent, unique in its requirements and
unparalleled in its potential. Like most adolescents it wants to be
accepted as an adult as it tries to pull away from its parents. If it is
going to reach its full potential, it must take a few lessons from the
more seasoned world of software development.

- -

Chapter 2 *Project Estimating*

Estimation is alchemy! We can't just add up the number of Web pages and functions and multiply by some level of complexity to get a magic answer. For years we tried to do this and ruined our businesses and customer relationships. XP offers a new way grounded in our day-to-day experiences. Better yet, with XP it is okay to be wrong.

Chapter 3 *Customer Trust*

Traditional Web development has always set up customers as the "others." They paid the bills but somehow they were a foreign entity intruding on development. Such segregation has consistently back-fired. Where developers wanted privacy they got scrutiny; where they wanted blind faith they got distrust. The walls that divide developers from customers sabotage the whole project. XP offers new practices of inclusion that might be hard to swallow at first but pay off immediately.

Chapter 4   *The Release Plan* 27

Creating a clear map of where the project is going is an important first step. It lets you identify risks, clarify objectives, and determine if the project even makes sense. The only thing more important than the Release Plan is not to take it too seriously.

Part II: Working on Web XP Projects 37

Chapter 5   *The Project Team* 39

Web projects use teams of multidisciplined professionals. Knowing what their responsibilities are and how they overlap with each other up front prevents fuctioning and infighting.

Chapter 6   *The Development Environment* 53

Web development environments have always stressed cool over functional. Where the team sat and how their spaces were arranged took second place to more important concerns about where to put the pool table or if the climbing wall was high enough. For XP to work you need to think about how the team interacts as a group and works as individuals.

Chapter 7   *Working in Iterations* 61

Web projects are traditionally done in waterfall style with define, design, develop, and deploy stages each taking months. These projects can be done more effectively and with less risk following short iterations of a couple of weeks.

Practices and documents that help the customer make small incremental decisions are a focus of XP and the foundation of our XP'd graphic design process.
With HTML we build brittle, unmaintainable sites. XML frees us to create fluid site architectures that are change friendly and easy to maintain. Pages are not objects yet, but we are getting close.

Design is not a phase of a project that gives way to a building phase. Design and creation are one and the same. XP stresses this interconnectedness and reduces the number of design documents to those that actually help developers develop.

Coding is not typing! Coding is problem solving.

Testing shouldn't wait until the project is finished. Start testing before you write one line of code. Test constantly and effectively and you will develop a much more durable Web site.

Foreword

Until now all of the noncompilation books on Extreme Programming (XP) have come from those of us who were involved in its birth. I am very happy that my friends and former clients have written the first book from the "second generation" of XP practitioners. When I first sat down with Doug Wallace, I could see that he already knew how to apply much of XP to his problem domain. This book represents that knowledge tempered by the heat of real projects.

I have spent most of my career working on back-office projects. Because our user interface was going to be used by clerical workers, our projects didn't have to be pretty. We really didn't care what they said about the company; they only had to contribute to our customer's efficiency. Our interfaces had to present large amounts of data, so we didn't waste screen real estate on fancy graphics. We certainly didn't spend much time thinking about aesthetics. During my career, I have written ugly screens in IMS/DC, CICS, Power-Builder, Smalltalk, and now in Java and TK.

It was a wonderful experience to work with a group whose job was caring what an interface "said." When Doug explained the process the creative group used, my first thought was, "This is already XP." It was all about simplicity, feedback, communication, and courage.

Doug Wallace, Isobel Raggett, and Joel Aufgang have written a book that applies our values to a slightly different problem space. Their team consists of not only software engineers and customers interested in functionality but marketing experts, graphic artists, writers, and copyeditors. They use pair programming to break down the walls that have traditionally separated the creative and engineering departments. They use automated testing on projects that were previously tested by eye. Finally, they use variable-scope contracts on projects that had always been done on a fixed-price basis.

As with the rest of Extreme Programming, this book represents a set of best practices that will allow a new set of developers to run with the dials turned up to ten. I think that represents a great step forward for XP and the software community.

Chet Hendrickson
Farmington Hills, Michigan

Preface

Estimating the time and the costs of Web projects has been my obsession for more than five years. Starting with wild guesstimates and little success, I was quickly attracted to the analysis practices of the Rational Process. I spent weeks with customers doing Use Cases and Activity Diagrams, trying to define the scope of a project. However, these specifications told me nothing about the work effort involved and led to huge fights with customers over the changes they inevitably wanted.

Three years ago I went to the Software Expo in San Jose and heard Martin Fowler talk about a new set of practices called XP, or Extreme Programming. I was hooked. XP let me acknowledge the futility of estimation. It taught me about the interconnectedness of price, time, scope, and quality and about the importance of letting the customer make continuous trade-offs between the four. XP changed the rules of how I, as a project manager, engaged with customers and overnight it improved my customer relationships and my bottom line.

If estimation was my obsession, then development was my curse. Every project seemed to be going fine and then stalled at 90 percent. It would take us three months to do 90 percent of the work and six months to do the last 10 percent. Once completed, the sites we were building were a nightmare to maintain, and I lost many good programmers who would rather abandon ship than babysit a mass of unintelligible, brittle code. Developing sites in iterations and using unit tests made a lot of sense but didn't translate naturally to Web development. While the pure coding server-side issues melded well with XP, we had client-side issues, graphic design issues, and serious conflicts in trying to use a practice meant for object-oriented systems on inherently non-object–oriented Web page architecture. If Web projects were going to use XP, then XP would have to change and so would the way Web sites were structured and developed.

Over the last two years, we have experimented with practices to get the most out of XP in a Web development environment. We have extended our practices to include graphic designers, interface programmers, copywriters, and the rest of the diverse team that goes into building a Web site. We have developed new design patterns for Web site creation using XML, Cascading Style Sheets, and XSLT to impose an architecture that better supports continuous integration and the separation of content, graphical design, and functionality.

We highly recommend that readers of this book first look at Kent Beck's original XP book, *Extreme Programming Explored*, to see the origins of the XP practices described here and to better see where his and our practices differ.

Acknowledgments

Many people helped us write this book. First we would like to thank all the clients who have taught us so much and all the teams who have shared in the learning—in particular, our team at Agile let us experiment on them and gave us so much feedback.

This is our first book, and we must thank our reviewers, Kent Beck, Frank Westphal, William Wake, Edward Hieatt, and Jessica Burdman for their help. Their input made us think about our assumptions and greatly strengthened the work. A special thank you goes to Chet Hendrickson, who not only reviewed the book but also was our original XP coach. Chet deserves much of the credit for the idea of adapting XP to Web projects.

If this book is readable, the credit must go to Pat Latham, who edited the first draft and did a great job of making three distinct voices sound like one.

Finally, thank you to our editor, Ross Venables, and all the people at Addison-Wesley who believed in the book and helped shepherd it from idea to completion.

Part I

XP and Web Projects

The Web development industry comprises many disciplines. It formed out of nothingness less than ten years ago, starting with a team of one "Webmaster." It has come to include teams of programmers, graphic designers, usability specialists, and project managers, to name a few, which represent very different ways of looking at projects. Some team members come from an advertising background, others from software, and still others from every imaginable walk of life. The partners in my first Web development company were a former architect and a physician.

Each discipline tried to bring its established practices to bear on its part of the development equation and in some cases impose them on other disciplines. In this part we look at how this affected the fledgling industry.

Extreme Programming (XP) is a software methodology that offers solutions for teams facing rapid change. Does it fit the needs of Web development? The short answer is sort of.

Chapter 1

Why the Web Industry Needs XP

We are all in the gutter, but some of us
are looking at the stars.
—Oscar Wilde

Web development is an adolescent, unique in its requirements and
unparalleled in its potential. Like most adolescents it wants to be
accepted as an adult as it tries to pull away from its parents. If it is
going to reach its full potential, it must take a few lessons from the
more seasoned world of software development.

In the bad old days, the Web industry was experiencing growing
pains in its progress toward maturity. Technologies were changing
under our feet, and we still hadn't developed best practices for completing projects. It seemed as though too many customers were paying for the industry to learn how to do things right. Not
surprisingly, there were a lot of unhappy customers, and it is always
the unhappy ones who seem to talk. As a result Web development

was developing a bad reputation. What were we doing wrong? Quite a few things, it appears:

- ✧ We tried to be all things to all customers with insufficient expertise.
- ✧ We often failed to deliver on time or on budget.
- ✧ We tended to develop adversarial customer relationships.
- ✧ Our projects didn't always meet customer expectations.

Trying to Be All Things to All Customers

Most Web firms evolved from a software or an advertising background, tacking on Web development as an additional service to customers. We have found that the industry is made of both strong

Wearing too many hats, trying to be all things to all customers, leads to bad projects.

technical shops that lack a solid understanding of branding and marketing issues, and strong design firms that are weak in technology and user interface. A 2000 Forrester Research report[1] on e-commerce integrators mirrors our findings, even in the largest Web development companies. It graded 150 Web developers and found that in the categories of marketing, strategy, design, technology, and business practices not one scored higher than 70 percent across the board and most scored much lower.

Projects Not Delivered on Time or on Budget

The Forrester report showd that project management was an area of overall weakness, with 80 percent of respondents indicating that their projects were delivered late and over budget. Finding good project managers was the bane of our existence for years. It seemed to be the hardest position to fill, with few candidates having relevant experience in project management or Web development or having strong customer skills. As you can imagine, the chances of launching a site on time became a matter of luck. To date, few developers have put into practice a project management methodology that accurately tracks and adjusts projects and takes into account the multi-disciplined nature of the industry.

Adversarial Customer/Developer Relationships

Traditionally projects were (in most cases still are) a fixed-price, fixed-deliverable agreement based on an initial estimate of the overall

1. Averby, Christine Spivey, and Paul Sonderegger, with Harley Manning, Julie Meriger, Aaron Hardisty, and Sadaf Roshon, *eCommerce Integrators Exposed*. Forrester Research, June 2000.

Customers and developers may come to "blows"
about expected deliverables.

work involved. However, the chances of developers being able to guess the costs of a project accurately were minimal, and the challenge was to make the project fit the estimate. This could only result in an adversarial relationship, in which the customer consistently took the widest interpretation of what was included and the developer responded with the narrowest, with both sides taking contrary positions on the expected deliverables. The inevitable changes to the project often caused bitter fights.

Unsuccessful Projects

Web companies consistently sought projects with larger budgets under the mistaken assumption that this would automatically boost their profits. But without defining the metrics for determining project success, they couldn't define the requirements and functionality that would signal project completion. Simply delivering a Web site on time was not enough. Moreover, unless it solved the customer's business challenges and/or provided a means to measure the impact of the site on the customer's business, it was not a successful project. Unfortunately, as projects made it to production the developers lost sight of the original objectives and wasted many expensive man hours on unnecessary or unwanted tasks because they forgot why they had been hired in the first place.

The XP Solution

After analyzing the mistakes the industry was making, we needed to come up with practical, cost-effective solutions. Clearly, Web development teams needed to adopt new development methodologies. These methodologies needed to stress customer involvement in the day-to-day decisions within the project, include incremental milestones of weeks rather than months, and allow for ongoing refinement of estimates based on actual progress. Project management would have to be redefined, not as software or advertising but as a new entity consisting of multidisciplined teams with close coupling to customer stakeholders.

We knew of XP in association with software development and wondered if it could solve the problems in Web development. Given the Web industry's essential differences from the software industry, could XP be as good a fit?

Web Development versus Software Development

XP methodology could potentially deal with a number of Web development problems. XP involves the customer, integrates teams, generates maintainable code, and, most important, divides the responsibility for project success between the developer and the customer and so creates an atmosphere of trust. But would XP map directly to the needs of Web projects? Extreme Programming was developed to resolve problems in software, not Web, development. There are a number of key differences between the two.

Teams

Web projects involve multidisciplinary teams made up of graphic designers, copywriters, Flash programmers, server-side programmers, interface programmers, testers, and project managers. Team members can't be isolated because decisions made by one affect the others, and the intersection and overlapping of skills make it impossible to set strict boundaries of responsibility. A series of questions and answers illustrates this:

Question: Who is responsible for how the page displays?
Answer: The designer and the interface programmer.

Question: Who is responsible for how a function works between the server and the customer?
Answer: The server-side programmer and the interface programmer.

Question: How does the Flash element pull a weather forecast from a third-party application?
Answer: Better ask the designer, the Flash developer, the interface programmer and the server-side programmer. Oh, and you'd better ask the customer about everything!

XP is very good at getting programmers to communicate among themselves and with customers. Web projects require a myriad of new disciplines. How does XP cope with this decision-making interconnectedness?

Support for Multiple User Environments

Most software projects create deliverables for one platform at a time. Different software versions are developed to handle different user environments. For example, the latest release of an application will have a version for Windows, a version for UNIX, and perhaps a version for Mac, depending on its audience. Unfortunately, in Web we don't have the luxury of separating out the product. There is only one version of the Web site, and it must be able to support multiple browsers on multiple operating systems simultaneously, running multiple screen color and resolution settings, not to mention modem speeds. Worse, not only do the system requirements vary depending on the Web site audience but they can change from the beginning of a project to the end.

How does Extreme Programming allow for the varied support needed in one product?

Testing

Web projects require unique testing practices to account for multiple customers, and they have an emphasis on how things look that is often unheard of in software projects. Testers have to be able to test interfaces in totally new ways. For example, page layout, design, screen colors, and screen resolution are all requirements that can be tested only by eye.

How does XP deal with the need for sense-based testing?

Rapid Deployment

Software developers have the luxury of large releases. The cost of a new version of the software forces the customer to plan releases carefully and to make them substantial revisions. Web projects can be deployed as often as the customer wants. Web XP projects need to harmonize continuous integration with new release practices.

How does XP accommodate the need for frequent deployment?

Customers

Software development needs a customer to set priorities, define the problem domain, and make key decisions, because it is the customer who understands the process that the software is trying to emulate. Web projects are generally the development of a corporate Web site or system and are often marketing vehicles new to the organization. Thus, it is hard to find an expert to consult. Web customers look to their developers for far more guidance than XP allows.

How can Extreme Programming help educate customers and increase customer satisfaction?

Quality

Many original Web sites were low-quality, brittle masses of code. Few Web developers used an object-oriented approach to development. Most used procedural languages, which made refactoring code or making changes to it much more difficult—often sites were simply redeveloped each time enough changes were requested. Over time sites get worse, not better. New design patterns pioneered for software have to be created for Web sites.

How can XP help to improve quality?

XP Web Development

In providing satisfactory answers to the questions just asked, XP has had a great influence on the way we have developed projects over the last two years. We have developed a number of mutations that serve our projects well and that make the use of XP for creating Web sites second nature to us. In many cases we have simply extended an XP practice to nonprogrammers; in others we have invented new practices.

In general we have found XP methods to be especially helpful in three key areas:

✦ Project estimating

✦ Customer relationships

✦ Release planning

Rather than define how Web projects should use XP, we will attempt to explain what has worked for us and to open the dialog between the Web development and XP communities.

Chapter 2

Project Estimating

No one can draw more out of things, books included,
than he already knows. A man has no ears for that
to which experience has given him no access.
—Friedrich Nietzsche

Estimation is alchemy! We can't just add up the number of Web pages
and functions and multiply by some level of complexity to get a magic
answer. For years we tried to do this and ruined our businesses and
customer relationships. XP offers a new way grounded in our day-
to-day experiences. Better yet, with XP it is okay to be wrong.

Web developers are no better at estimation than software developers are. In fact, given the multiskilled team requirements for Web projects, only the very best project managers have even a clue about how long something will take. Nevertheless, Web companies have tried a variety of estimation techniques, such as:

- ❖ Equations
- ❖ Man hours

✧ Fixed-price quotes

✧ Past projects

The Pitfalls of Estimating

None of the techniques just listed has worked well. Ladies and gentlemen, as we said, estimation is alchemy. Now we will tell you why.

Equations

For some reason people think that you can estimate the cost of a project using equations. We have seen people add up the total number of pages and the total number of queries and then multiply by some percentage based on how troublesome the sales team thinks

There are no "magic" formulas for estimating project development time and costs.

the customer will be. We have also seen attempts to calculate how much business value the project will add.

Fixed-Price Quotes

Fixed-price quotes take you out of the Web development business and into the insurance business—you are assuming the customer's risk. That is what the money is for, not the deliverable. Time and expense arrangements, on the other hand, put all the risk onto the customer, making them very hard to sell.

Past Projects

Basing a cost estimate on a past, similar project is, in our experience, the worst estimation technique there is. Ask a programmer, graphic designer, or tester how long something will take and the estimates on the whole will be far less than they should be. This is because our memories tend to shrink time.

The Parameters of Estimating

How much a project will cost depends on four main factors, all of them interrelated:

- Time to deliver
- Price
- Scope
- Quality

Time

The best way to lose a customer is to promise to build her site in half the time and not tell her that it will be brittle, it will be impossible to maintain, and it will slow to a crawl under a heavy load. She may love you when you deliver, but within six months will tell you that you will never work for her again. Worse, she will expect you to maintain her site during that six months, and your team will hate you because you made them bail water and plug holes in a sinking ship for half a year.

Price

If the customer needs a Web site in three months instead of five, the cost must increase or the quality or scope must decrease. The only way to get a job done faster is to increase the size of the team or work longer hours, and both solutions have their limits. Only so many people can work on a project at one time, and people can only work extra hours in short bursts or they burn out and become less effective. You can reduce quality but only so far, and be assured that you are going to pay for the reduced quality sooner than you think. The only safe bet is to reduce scope and do less.

Scope

In the past scope shrank if it wasn't defined in enough detail at the beginning of the project. If it wasn't written in the original contract, in a way that all parties understood, it meant that there was some mythical leeway.

Unfortunately, this far too common practice of building the least possible amount of functionality led to some very unhappy customers, simply because they didn't get to decide. If the customer asked for a newsletter, the developers would ask themselves what features made up a newsletter and which ones could be dropped while still technically delivering what was requested.

The only time dropping features is good is when the customer is the one deciding which ones.

Quality

In traditional Web development methodologies, quality was poor because it was the easiest factor to ignore. Customers need to be educated about the work you do so that they can fully understand the implications of ignoring quality. Some customers have great difficulty understanding what quality means. You need to take the time to explain that skipping steps introduces bugs into the design and that rushing turns code into spaghetti. Of all the things you can do to a developer, making her responsible for bad code and poor design when the customer will not allow sufficient time is the worst.

An XP Estimating Strategy

During seven years of building Web sites, we have tried many techniques to improve the accuracy of our estimates. One reason we were attracted to XP in the first place was the concept of breaking down the work so that estimates could be based on smaller iterations. After all, the reason you can't quote a project accurately is that you have no idea what it will be until you are done.

So how does XP improve project cost estimation? It reduces the risk of fixed-price quotes, and it provides better track of man hours required for project tasks.

Less Risk on Fixed-Price Quotes

XP takes much of the risk out of fixed price quoting. As we have seen, most customers require a fixed-price quote and are unhappy with anything more open ended. You will usually have no choice but to go this route. However, XP shares the risk by making the customer commit to paying for the man hours used but only one iteration at a time. Other contractual arrangements may be made to ensure the customer's commitment to the project, but in essence the customer is on the hook for the iteration although he can leave at any time.

Better Time Tracking

XP relies on estimating using "yesterday's weather"; that is, if it was 75°F yesterday, it will probably be 75°F today. With subtle adjustments for variance, this method will produce a relaxed curve from summer to winter. The same is true of projects. If a graphical designer can cut up to 20 buttons in an hour one day, he can most likely do the same number the next day.

The best way to improve this is to track how long it actually takes to complete a task. For each task an estimate is collected, for which you need to record

✧ Who estimated the hours

✧ What they estimated

✧ How long the task really took

When similar tasks come up, remind the development team of their previous estimates. This will help them see trends in their estimates and improve them. When you compare the work actually done in a day to the estimate for it, the estimates for the next day become better. It's that easy.

You can see that the use of XP in project cost estimation can favorably affect a developer's bottom line. There will be much less risk of poor estimates that result in little or no profit or, worse, a loss. The advantage for customers lies is that they know exactly what they will get for what cost. Better estimation increases customer trust.

Chapter 3

Customer Trust

Before you trust a man, eat a peck of salt with him.
—Proverb

Traditional Web development has always set up customers as the "others." They paid the bills but somehow they were a foreign entity intruding on development. Such segregation has consistently backfired. Where developers wanted privacy they got scrutiny; where they wanted blind faith they got distrust. The walls that divide developers from customers sabotage the whole project. XP offers new practices of inclusion that might be hard to swallow at first but pay off immediately.

Promises Unkept

There are far too many Web development horror stories, and over the last seven years each of us has walked customers through some serious trust issues raised by a previous developer. This is not an easy process, but it is definitely worth it. Customer trust is everything, but in traditional web development methodologies, such as they were, it was difficult to cultivate. It was as if the best project managers were those who were best at lying to customers about the status of the project. In fact, the reverse should be true.

Keeping the customer out of the development
process destroys trust.

Early Web projects would start with a honeymoon phase, when the developer was first hired. Then the customer would request changes to the project, content development would lag, and developers would begin to worry about their estimates and how much functionality was promised. As the project started to slip, disagreements would develop on what was and what wasn't included in the project.

Then would come the divorce, sometimes before project completion, often immediately after the Web site launch. This meant that either the developer would be stuck with outstanding work to complete or that the customer would have no support or maintenance for its site. Not surprisingly, customers rarely awarded any more contracts to that developer. If the developer did stick to completing what the customer perceived as outstanding work, this would generally bite deeply into any project profit. Nobody was happy.

The most likely reasons for the falling out between customer and developer were

- ✧ Financial and estimating problems

- ✧ Failure to deliver on time

- ✧ Poor quality of work or poor communication

Financial and Estimating Problems

As described in the following sections, money problems were a factor for three main reasons.

Competition

The Web development industry was incredibly competitive, with thousands of development companies springing up in basements everywhere, forcing down prices and project quotes. Beyond a handful of publicly traded, "million-dollar-minimum-project" companies, however, the rest competed on an even playing field, and customers could not see the quality differences between two developers in a basement and a seasoned team of 20. This situation is now improving, with customers who have had bad experiences beginning to understand why and realizing they were comparing apples to oranges.

Such a change in attitude is a slow process. During the fevered dot-com days, development conditions never improved because, despite the failures, salaries continued to increase. Indeed, there was a time when a programmer with six months' experience and a basic grasp of Visual Basic could demand and get $60K to $70K a year.

Bad Estimates

Web project estimates were horrendous because many Web developers were cowboys or heroes. Projects often depended on programmers running in at the end and saving the day by working crazy hours to finish. Unfortunately, many of them used this as the basis for all time estimates going forward. If you asked, "How long would it take to build an atomic bomb?" they would actually have an answer: "Oh, I could do it in a day or two if I had to." This misguided optimism obviously compounded the problem of estimating.

In the early days of Web programming, developers were asked to write code that created simple things like web counters or display of a list of products from a database. We just used simple tools and unfortunately got used to them, much like working with duct tape and glue. The problem was that many larger projects continued to use these same technologies in the belief that the large projects were more of the same thing, just bigger. The idea that complexity would grow the project exponentially took the industry too long to learn. Developers cut their own throats by quoting far less than the project was worth and didn't find out how badly off they were until three quarters of the way through.

Poorly Defined Requirements

Web project requirements were poorly defined. Some projects started with flimsy functional requirements at best, which caused many problems. Most customers agreed to a fixed price for a fixed deliverable; however, most deliverables couldn't be defined up front, so the fixed price became less definite. Customers took the widest interpretation of the project scope and developers began to realize that they had to take the leanest interpretation to stay afloat. Customers were thus left out of the development process in an attempt to reduce change requests and only brought in for major milestones. This led to their devaluing the work that was being done by the developers.

Failure to Deliver

Not only were projects delivered late but they were often not what the customer wanted. Insufficient customer involvement meant that the development team was making crucial decisions, without customer input, about how things should work, what was important, and what things should look like. This often meant that the development team, not the customer, was essentially making business decisions with little or no understanding of the customer's business processes and goals. Customers were receiving their Web sites months late and what was delivered wasn't what they thought they had initially requested.

Poor Quality and Communications

Quality was difficult to measure, especially by customers. Customers rarely appreciated the quality that went into a well-built Web site because they couldn't see it. They couldn't see that the naming conventions were adhered to, that code was properly commented, or that functions had robust error-handling capabilities. Nor could they see that the designers had spent time reducing the file sizes of the graphics so that they would download faster or that the programmers had spent countless hours trying to ensure that the design of the Web site appeared consistent across multiple browsers.

Unfortunately, because the customer couldn't see the results of hours of high-quality development, it was often the first thing to be dropped from the project. However, poor quality wasn't hard for customers to see and they were not happy to pay for it. Even if they did pay for it, every battle they won for extra scope somewhere led to the developer secretly making up time by reducing quality somewhere else.

In time, customers would experience the effects of poor quality but their developer would refuse to offer maintenance contracts for ongoing changes. New developers would recommend rebuilding the Web site as this was most cost-effective solution, leading to the customer feeling betrayed by previous and current developers and resenting the money "wasted" on the Web site. This breakdown in communications was a clear recipe for disaster.

Building Trust

As you can imagine, all of these problems contributed to a complete lack of trust and respect on both sides, which gave the Web industry a clear challenge: How could it avoid all these problems?

A Customer Bill of Rights

A good relationship with a customer is based on trust. By following XP best practices, we can build that trust and avoid most of the problems just discussed. With Web XP the customer will become more involved in the project and will be able to make decisions along the way. The iterative nature of XP allows customers to trust you for a couple of weeks at a time. Being fully involved in the planning process, they know what you are going to do and why. They also have greater influence over what is done, and when, than ever before. In the process they learn about how quality, scope, price, and time are interconnected and *they*, not you, start making the trade-offs.

Customer participation to this degree amounts to a customer Bill of Rights, first put forward by Ron Jeffries, one of the early pioneers of XP. The following sections describe a practical Bill of Rights for Web projects that helps build and maintain trust.

The Right to an Overall Plan

Customers have the right to a release plan that outlines what can be done, when, and at what cost.[1] They have the right go through the development of that plan with you. How do you get customers and developers to agree on what is included in a project? You develop iteratively and agree in small pieces. This means developing a plan for every iteration of work. The iteration plan has to be detailed enough to describe what is to be done, when, and for how much.[2]

The Right to Make Changes

Customers will change their minds—substitute functionality and alter priorities—and shouldn't have to pay exorbitant prices to do so. It is the nature of any Web project that, before the Web site is launched,

---

1. See Chapter 4 for a full discussion of release planning.
2. Chapter 7 contains a full treatment of the iterative process.

something will change that. At the beginning of each iteration, give the customer the opportunity to change direction by requesting new stories or reevaluating story priorities. (See Chapter 7.)

The Right to Get Value

Customers should receive the greatest possible value out of every development week. While they are paying for your time, they are also paying for your experience and good-quality work. Engage customers in the process—let them see what you are doing.

The Right to See Progress

Customers should be able to view a running system at the end of each iteration. At the beginning of each iteration, a set of stories is approved. For each story a provable deliverable is defined, which is what the customer will review at the end of each iteration to determine that the story is complete. This can be done by running the code and having it pass repeatable tests.

A customer Bill of Rights breaks down the walls between the customer and the team and builds trust.

The Right to Be Informed

The project manager and team members should have regular access to customers in order to keep them informed. Communication is critical to the project, as it gives customers a chance to become more involved in development of the Web site and therefore more able to make key decisions along the way. Don't hide from customers. Keep them involved in everyday project development. If something comes up tell them right away; don't procrastinate. It is their right to determine the impact of a problem, and only they can say what an acceptable solution should be.

The Customer Bill of Rights as a Selling Point

A customer Bill of Rights makes an excellent selling point for any Web developer. It sends two important messages to a potential customer:

- ✧ You are confident in the abilities of your company to deliver a good product.

- ✧ You respect the customer's expertise in his own business and value the contribution he will make to the project.

Chapter 4

The Release Plan

*Just because something doesn't do what you
planned it to, does not mean it's useless.*
—Thomas Edison

*Creating a clear map of where the project is going is an important
first step. It lets you identify risks, clarify objectives, and determine
if the project even makes sense. The only thing more important
than the Release Plan is not to take it too seriously.*

Release planning is creating a game plan for your Web project
outlining what you think you want your Web site to be. The plan is
a guide for the content, design elements, and functionality of a Web
site to be released to the public, to partners, or internally. It also
estimates how long the project will take and how much it will cost.
What the plan is not is a functional specification that defines the
project in detail or that produces a budget you can take to the bank.

Basically you use a Release Plan to do an initial sanity check of the
project's feasibility and worthiness. Release Plans are useful road maps,
but don't think of them as guides to the interstate road system.

It's always a good idea to have a map of where
a project is headed.

Instead, think of them as the maps used by early explorers—half
rumor and guess and half hope and expectation.

Generating a Release Plan is as much an exercise in customer
relations as it is the writing of a document. Web project requirements seem fairly loose to begin with, so simply spending a day with
the customer usually isn't enough to get all the information you
need. If you want a happy customer, you need to firm up information in at least four key areas:

✧ What the customer is hoping to achieve through the
  Web site

✧ What the best strategies are to achieve those goals

✧ What technical constraints apply to the target audience
  for the site

✧ What Web technologies are most appropriate

There are no easy answers to writing the release plan, but here is the process we have found most effective in producing successful projects. Keep it short and cover only the important issues. XP is not about generating documents.

Customer Goals

We start the process by scheduling three meetings with the customer, each approximately three hours in length. The main objective of these meetings is to thrash out what the customer should be doing online. We review what other companies have done in this area (including key competitors), what possibilities there are for our customer, and what new ideas should be discussed further.

Each meeting focuses on one of the following topics:

- The Internet as a tool to reach the public
- The Internet as a tool to reach partners and suppliers
- The Internet as a tool for internal collaboration

The strategist or project manager will begin each meeting with a presentation aimed at educating the participants on the relevant issues and best practices of other Internet projects currently online in the topic area.[1] More than just background reviews to bring the customer up to speed, the meetings are also a basis for discussion.

Customers don't have the experience to tell the development team what they want. They need a coach to educate them on the business opportunities and pitfalls of the proposed Web-based site or system. Good strategists will lay out the full range of what can be done to make the site a success in the marketplace. The customer

---

1. See Chapter 5 for a full discussion of project team roles and responsibilities.

still calls all the shots, and, as she becomes more aware of the development and business issues, the role of the strategist diminishes.

Once the presentation is complete, the meeting turns to answering a number of questions prepared by the strategist. These questions, intended to spark conversation and aid in brainstorming, include

- ✦ What are the goals of the project?

- ✦ What metrics can be used to determine the success of the project?

- ✦ What impact can this project have on parallel projects?

- ✦ What are the development priorities for content and functions?

- ✦ What constraints are there on the technology and design of the Web site(s)?

- ✦ What is the structure of the customer's existing business processes?

- ✦ What required content should be incorporated into the Web site or Web-based system?

- ✦ What is the nature of the existing content? Can a list of this content be created?

- ✦ What level of involvement does the customer want in the creation of any or all new content?

Release plan meetings are crucial because they raise customer awareness about what can be done on the Web. Many developers skip this step and instead use their own knowledge about the Internet and the customer's company in a proposal. This is a mistake because you don't know what the customer's real issues are. You can help by giving the customer enough information about what is possible, but he is in the best position to judge. In our experience the time spent educating the customer in things you take for granted transforms him into a team member.

It is also important to ensure that the customer is represented at meetings by all of those who will have crucial input into the strategic questions to be raised. Many companies involve only the marketing department or just the IT department in these talks, but we always push for representation from both. We have spent days in meetings to define projects with marketing departments, only to find that the proposed solution will require software that is not approved by IT. We have also worked with IT departments that agonize over which browsers to support for an internal application, only to have marketing tell them that they can mandate the use of just one.

Strategies for Achieving Customer Goals

Once everyone is clear on what the customer is trying to achieve, you can discuss what direction the customer should take and what type of content areas will appear on the site. Several options will arise that the customer has expressed interest in. The next step is to evolve these options into several concepts, which may include

- ✧ Providing product training for vendors, retailers, or staff
- ✧ Providing newsletter registration and mailing to contact interested prospects/customers
- ✧ Providing live chat for online customer support

Defining these directions requires further work. This may include research on the potential idea to find out how feasible it is. Has it been tried elsewhere? If so, how successful was it? Sometimes further input from the customer may be required.

Technical Constraints

The next step is to define constraints for the project. You need to make the customer aware that constantly changing technology will inevitably involve some constraints on how potential audiences view the site. This work will include reviewing the Web logs for the customer's existing site and further analysis of recent trends. Items to be defined include the user environment information in the following list.

- What percentage of the target audience is using each of the following operating systems?
  - Mac OS 8.6, 9.0, 9.1, 9.2, X
  - Windows 95, 98, 2000, NT, XP
  - Other

- What percentage of the target audience is using each of the following browsers?
  - Netscape 4.77, 6
  - Microsoft Internet Explorer 4.0, 5.0, 5.5, 6.0
  - Other

- What percentage of the target audience is using each of the following screen colors?
  - 8 bit (256 colors)
  - 16 bit (65,536 colors)
  - 24 bit (16,777,216 colors)

- What percentage of the target audience is using each of the following screen resolutions?
  - 585 by 386 pixels (AOL TV)
  - 640 by 480 pixels
  - 800 by 600 pixels
  - 1,024 by 768 pixels

- 1,152 by 864 pixels
- 1,280 by 1024 pixels

✦ What percentage of the target audience and what percentage of access are connecting at each of the following connection speeds?
- 14.4K baud or less
- 28.8K baud
- 33.6K baud
- 56.6K baud
- 128K baud

✦ What percentage of the target audience has installed each of the following plug-ins?
- LiveAudio
- Flash
- AVI
- QuickTime
- Beatnik
- RealPlayer G2
- Acrobat
- ShockWave
- MediaPlayer

From this research, try to assess what the minimum requirements are by analyzing the percentages. If any platforms, browsers, and applications are being used by more than 10 percent of your audience, they should be supported; if used by less than 10 percent but greater than 5 percent, look at the trends. If it is an older technology, chances are that it will be decreasing in usage and that it shouldn't be recommended. If it is a new technology, chances are that these numbers are only going to increase and supporting it may be a good idea.

Unfortunately, supporting multiple applications isn't an exact science. You probably learned this when you tried to line up graphics to appear the same in Internet Explorer and Netscape. For this reason you should note which is the most popular technology and focus on supporting that first. Make the customer aware that other applications that the Web site should support may not appear exactly the same way. The Web site will be as functional, but it may look a little different. Don't feel bad about this; you can't control the fact that HTML is interpreted differently from browser to browser and platform to platform. Just make sure that the customer is aware of this from the start.

Appropriate Web Technologies

While many companies work on technologies on their own, we like to involve the customer. We start by walking him through the various languages and frameworks that can be employed, describing the benefits and drawbacks of each. It is worth the effort to provide a one-hour presentation on the advantages of an object-oriented language, the need for clustering, and the relative merits of Oracle and SQL Server to marketing customers. These are decisions that the customer should participate in making. Never assume otherwise because the choice of technologies used in Web site development will affect the lifecycle of the Web site, ongoing maintenance costs, and other real business concerns.

The Release Plan Document

The Release Plan document that is generated from all of these exercises includes

⬦ A description of the target audience

- Constraints of technologies and supported customers
- Site function and contents
- A site map outlining site structure and navigation
- Working titles for sections
- An estimated budget and timeline

The budget and timeline estimates are given in man hours, and a man week is assumed to be 25 hours long. (You can pick your own number to define a man week. Ours comes from our experience that an average person working 40 hours a week can be expected to do 25 hours of actual customer work. Some do more and some do less.) This benchmark is our expected individual velocity.

Velocity is an important concept in XP.[2] Some measure it by how many function points—individual pieces of functionality—are done in an iteration, but function points are difficult in Web projects because not everything is a function.[3] On Web projects time is the only common denominator between the various disciplines. We will deal with velocity in detail later, but for now understand it as the work effort you commit to. To every iteration you are committing a certain amount of scope. Using the number of hours you are in the office as a guide to how much work can be accomplished is a quick way to get in trouble. Velocity is all about being realistic about what can be done in an iteration and determining how large a team you will need.

We give the customer multiple scenarios in the Release Plan for various team sizes and for soft dates for launching the site to a

---

2. Project velocity is discussed in Chapter 11.
3. Think of function points as the atoms that make up the application; for example, writing data to a file.

review group and to the public. For Web projects here are some helpful metrics for estimation:

✧ Take 20 percent of the developers' hours for project management; that is, if the total developers' hours are 100, then 20 hours is the approximate project management time.

✧ Take 20 percent of the developers' hours for testing; that is, if the total developers' hours are 100, then 20 hours is the approximate testing time.

One big advantage of involving the customer in release planning is that you will have less explaining to do once the plan is presented to the customer and the customer will have a sense of ownership of the document. This can have an enormous impact on the project success.

Part II

Working on Web XP Projects

Part I was about facing the issues of Web development. Part II is about solutions. Here we will look at teams, the environment they work in, how they work together, and how to plan for and execute a Web iteration.

While Part I described a world that we all know well, now we describe a world that is foreign, in which the basic precepts of how Web teams interrelate and tackle projects are challenged.

Special attention will be given to the pieces that don't come under traditional XP, such as graphic design.

Chapter 5

The Project Team

Our military forces are one team—in the game to win regardless of who carries the ball. This is no time for "fancy dans" who won't hit the line with all they have on every play, unless they can call the signals.
—General Omar Bradley

Web projects use teams of multidisciplined professionals. Knowing what their responsibilities are and how they overlap with each other up front prevents factioning and infighting.

The worst thing about any job is not knowing what you are supposed to do. Defining someone's job means that they actually know what they are responsible for, what you expect of them, and what they don't have to worry about. With roles and responsibilities for team members defined, projects run much more smoothly and team morale improves. The question is, how do roles in typical XP projects fit roles required in typical Web development projects and how do people work together in the context of iterative development and continuous integration? To answer these questions we need to take a look at the following:

The worst thing about any job is not knowing what
is expected of you.

- ✦ What roles are in a typical XP project
- ✦ What roles are in a typical Web development project
- ✦ How our experiment in paired development strategy worked
- ✦ Team work in continuous integration

Typical XP Project Roles

Here are some of the main roles that have been suggested in the XP literature.

- ✦ The *manager* schedules the iteration meetings, ensures that the process is being followed, provides reporting, and removes project obstacles.
- ✦ The *customer* writes and prioritizes user stories (think of stories as ideas for features; see Chapter 7) and writes acceptance criteria. She has the authority to make decisions.

- The *coach* oversees the entire project to ensure that the team is following XP best practices.

- The *tracker* tracks the teams' progress, helping them solve problems and warning the manager of any potential problems.

- The *programmer* estimates stories, breaking them up into tasks and estimating tasks; volunteers for stories; and writes unit tests.

- The *tester* helps the customer write acceptance criteria, writes and runs functional tests, and reports test results.

- The *doomsayer*, or naysayer, is anyone on the team who senses a problem and brings it to the attention of the team. (Let's hope it isn't always the tester.)

By the way, the doomsayer role is symbolic and played by different people at different times. When someone points out a problem, she needs to be heard without feeling like a negative influence. In standup meetings (see Chapter 10), it is common for someone to play doomsayer and lay out a problem the rest of the team would rather not see. Everyone gripes, but when the gripe is prefaced with "I need to be the doomsayer for a minute," everyone stops and listens. doomsayer should be a role of great power.

For more information on all team roles, read Chapter 22 of *Extreme Programming Explained*.[1]

Web XP Project Roles

Unfortunately, Web development is subtly different from typical XP projects, and therefore these roles need to be modified for it. For example, while one of the fundamentals of XP states that team

---

1. Beck, Kent. *Extreme Programming Explained*. Boston: Addison-Wesley, 2000.

Web XP development teams are made up of individuals with various roles, each having its own challenges.

members shouldn't specialize, specialization is inevitable in Web development. The following sections describe some of the main roles that we have found necessary in Web XP.

Customer

This role has been clearly defined as the person who "writes the user stories and specifies functional tests. Sets priorities, explains stories, views CRC sessions. . . . May or may not be an end user. Has authority to decide questions about the stories."[2] Web customers range widely in their knowledge of

✧ What the Web site needs to do

✧ The Internet and computers in general

✧ The XP process

---

2. See *http://c2.com/cgi/wiki?ExtremeProgrammingCorePractices*.

If Web XP is to work, there needs to be accommodations for customers with varying abilities and experience. What we recommend is a series of training sessions at the beginning of the project for those who are unfamiliar with the Internet and what it can do and on XP and what, as customers, they will be responsible for.

Customers need to learn how to write user stories and how to prioritize them. They start by accepting or rejecting user stories developed by team members and assigning priorities. Then they go on to write their own stories depending on their comfort level. Customers also accept whether stories have been completed. The tester works side by side with the customer to write acceptance criteria for each story.

Strategist

For customers who are unfamiliar with XP and uncomfortable with writing user stories, the strategist will play a key role. He is the primary customer advisor, training them on writing stories by translating their business requirements into stories that the team can develop. In a way the strategist becomes the customer's XP coach. Another part of the strategist's responsibility is to be the customer's advocate.

Developer

There are many different types of developer who work on Web projects, including interface programmers, server-side programmers, graphic designers, and flash developers. They are responsible for showing up for daily standup meetings and iteration planning meetings, suggesting stories to the customer, estimating stories, defining and estimating tasks, and volunteering for and completing tasks.[3]

Interface Programmer

The interface programmer's main responsibility is to translate how each Web page should look and to program the interface. She

---

3. See Chapter 11 for a full discussion of project planning.

works with the graphic designer to define the Web site's Cascading Style Sheet (CSS) and programs the lay out. This programming is primarily in XSLT, JavaScript, and other client-side languages. Whether the page is static text or an output of a server-side application, the interface programmer is responsible for every page.[4]

Graphic Designer

The graphic designer is responsible for the look of every page on the site. By following the graphic design process (see Chapter 8), she prepares mockups of the home page and an inside page. She then works with the interface programmer to lay out individual page content and functionality and to design the CSS.

Server-Side Programmer

The responsibilities of the server-side programmer are very close to those of the traditional XP programmer. He programs all server-side functionality and works with the interface programmer on any interfaces for application outputs.

Can someone be a server-side programmer and an interface programmer? Yes and no. Many programmers have the skills to do both, and if they don't at first they quickly will. These two roles work together often, and the transfer of skills is natural. Still, if staffing permits, we like to keep them as separate jobs. The worst Web sites are those that blur the lines between the client and server sides. Many programmers put SQL code right on a Web page. These direct calls to the database are the worst for making a site brittle. Server-side programmers should pretend that there is no Web site—for all they should care, the client is a cell phone or a flying car. Interface programmers should forget all about databases and treat the server as a black box that gives them what they need when they need it. Both worlds have more then enough on their plate to keep them busy and intrigued.

---

4. Chapter 8 contains a full treatment of the graphic design process.

Mentor

A role defined in XP is the tracker, one of whose responsibilities is to check in with the programmers and mentor their development. Since a Web development production staff includes different types of developers, the tracker must be able to mentor different skill sets. Finding a person to fill this type of position can be difficult, so we have divided this role into two main parts: technical lead for the interface programmers and server-side programmers and creative director for the graphic designers.

Mentors are responsible for all tracker tasks. "A mentor goes around a time or two a week, asks each programmer how she's doing, listens to the answer, takes action if things seem to be going off track. Actions include suggesting a CRC session, setting up a meeting with a customer, asking a coach or another programmer to help." [5]

We recommend that mentors be involved in production by volunteering for tasks, attending daily standup meetings, and estimating stories. They should also be more involved in the planning of an iteration (see Chapter 7) by suggesting stories to the customer and advising her on recommended priorities.

Project Manager

The XP manager role is very close to that of project manager, with both responsible for keeping iterations on schedule through iteration meetings, daily standup meetings, and customer meetings. Managers check in with the mentors to assess potential problems and notify customers when a story should be dropped from an iteration.

Managers also are responsible for removing any obstacles to development, whether by arranging for purchases, getting an answer from a customer, or improving team morale. Finally, they provide reports on the progress of each iteration and collect timesheets.

---

5. See *http://c2.com/cgi/wiki?ExtremeProgrammingCorePractices*.

When everyone knows what's expected of them and what
to expect from others, it's easy to find the way.

Tester (Quality Assurance)

In XP it is assumed that most of the testing will be unit tests, but this isn't so in Web development. Here much of the testing involves user interface elements that can't be automated. For example, should a button read "Next" or "Continue" and should it be aligned to the left or to the center of the page?

The tester is responsible for manually testing the user interface, writing acceptance tests with the customer, running manual or automated acceptance tests, reporting on errors, and allowing/not allowing a release out to the customer preview site.[6]

---

6. Chapter 14 discusses testing in Web XP projects.

Pair Programming

We first heard about pair programming—one of the pillars of XP—at a conference a couple of years ago. It sounded like a great idea, but we just couldn't believe that the developers we worked with would really agree to try it. However, after staying late one night to work on a defect report with a couple of programmers, one of us had a revelation. There we were, a project manager, an HTML programmer, and a Java programmer trying to make a page load and print the same way in Netscape and MSIE. After spending a few hours working on the problem separately, we ended up huddled around a computer, each making suggestions and each taking a turn at the keyboard. Within 30 minutes we solved the problem and each of us had learned something about the others and our various skills.

Now what if it wasn't just an HTML guy and a Java guy? In Web development there are different skills and knowledge to be shared. Wouldn't it be great if we could expand the pair programming technique to other areas of the project? For starters, imagine how much better Web sites would be if the graphic designers understood how pages are put together and how browsers can limit or expand the implementation of a design?

We started experimenting. First we tried pairing up interface programmers with backend developers. The results we got were what we expected:

- The programmers were happier and the morale of the team improved.

- Everyone learned a lot from his or her partners.

- The quality of the code was improved.

- There was less cowboy programming and more efficient code.

Then we tried to mix up the teams a bit more by combining different skill sets:

✧ Interface programmers with graphic designers

✧ Customers with testers

✧ Testers with graphic designers

✧ Customers with everyone

Out of each pairing came a better process and interesting results, described in the following sections.

Interface Programmers and Graphic Designers

Style documents were designed to define the same information that the CSS defines. The graphic designer/interface programmer pair could skip developing and then translating them into CSS by developing the CSS together. This gave the graphic designer more creative control and helped him understand the possibilities, making the design and interface better. We found that the CSS made a much better style document than anything we had created before.

Before the pairing, the graphic designer would create paper prototypes of the site, which became a set of instructions for the interface programmer. Yes, that meant a mockup of every page of the Web site, which the interface programmer would translate into XSLT. This would work only if the designer had a thorough understanding of the application's functionality and data and what the browsers supported. Instead, the graphic designer and interface programmer worked page by page, taking the XML schema, content, and tasks to develop the XSLT.[7] This change once again gave the graphic designer a better understanding of what was possible and improved the quality of the design.

---

7. See Chapter 10 for a full discussion of XML and XSLT.

As for customer approval, we found it was easier to create a PDF of the Web site for the customer than to print each of the Photoshop files that made up the mockup. It was also easier to make changes and keep documentation up to date.

Customers and Testers

Many customers we worked with had no experience writing acceptance criteria. By pairing them with testers, they became more comfortable with the process and hence created better criteria. This pairing also helped the testers develop better acceptance tests.

Testers and Graphic Designers

One of the hardest things to test is something subjective, like the interface to a Web site. That is why math was many people's favorite class in school—it is either right or wrong. Testers and graphic designers can develop tests for the Web site's layout, colors, fonts, and anything that can be defined. With this pairing we found that the tests developed were much better, and we were able to reduce the number of defects that carried the tag "But check with the designer to see if she wanted it this way."

Customers and Everyone

The more we made the customer a member of the team, the more he got involved in the process and the project and hence the more he enjoyed working with us. He trusted us more—the programmers weren't just tech guys in a back room he would never meet. He got to work with everyone, state opinions, and learn more about the steps involved in each task. We even started writing tasks that the customer would volunteer for and pair up with the team members on, such as collecting product data.

Continuous Integration

The following sections describe how XP continuous integration fosters teamwork on a Web development project.

Checking in Work

Everyone on our team is encouraged to check in their work often, at least once, and preferably many times, a day. All work, from code to graphics to content, is added to the repository. Once a new piece of work is checked in, we have a script that compiles any object code and then deploys to a development directory on the Web server, where another script runs all the automated tests we have written. The results of this build are published to a Web page.

Before we had this automated procedure, a team member would call out that she had checked in and the designated builder, often the project manager, would do the build manually. The automated system is more efficient, but sometimes we miss the sound of people calling out. It gave the shop an atmosphere of accomplishment.

Keeping on Track

Continuous integration protects the project from going too far off track. That is why, when the build breaks, we fix it immediately. What breaks a Web build? In addition to the unit tests we run a link checker, a spell checker, a code checker, and a page-size measuring tool.

A build fails if

- ✧ A unit test fails
- ✧ A spelling error occurs
- ✧ A missing page is found in the site
- ✧ A link is broken

- ✧ The parsed XML is not valid HTML

- ✧ The page is larger than an agreed on size

Any of these things can require someone to go back and fix his work. In Web XP, builds give feedback to the whole team and make everyone's work better.

Transitioning the Team to XP

In the transition to the XP process, there may be some hesitation. Some developers will be nervous about having the customer around while they work. Some may be wary of working in pairs. Some may not agree with writing unit tests first.

If you are experiencing resistance, you need to ask the team why they are dismissing these practices. Here are some likely answers.

"I don't want to pair-program with another developer—it will waste my time." Too many developers have tried and liked pair programming to dismiss it outright. We have worked with people who hated the idea at first but came around to its benefits. They found that it isn't a power struggle over the keyboard; it is working on solving a problem together. You need to remind foot draggers that they have to try it before they condemn the idea.

"I don't like having the customer around—he will just get in the way and make me uncomfortable." There is a common belief that customers are evil creatures who cause of all of a project's problems. This isn't true. Some of our best experiences on projects have been when the customer was sitting several feet away at his own desk, available to answer our questions, participate in setting priorities, and generally helping to inspire us. He actually became part of the team. This may seem like a leap of faith for developers, but it is a necessary one.

"I don't want to write unit tests—they sound like a lot of work and a waste of time." In practice, writing unit tests improves the quality of the work as well as the ease of maintenance. Every programmer's worst nightmare is having to take on someone else's work and make changes to it. By writing unit tests, you can make changes and know immediately what problems will occur. Once developers get into the habit of writing unit tests first, they will find that the process is not as cumbersome as they originally thought.

Whatever the excuses for avoiding XP, they usually dissolve over time. After the initial transition, people start to see XP's value and believe in its practices. There are companies that specialize in helping developers through this transition; they might be worth considering if you feel there is too much resistance.

Chapter 6

The Development Environment

Give us the tools and we'll finish the job.
—Winston Churchill

Web development environments have always stressed cool over functional. Where the team sat and how their spaces were arranged took second place to more important concerns about where to put the pool table or if the climbing wall was high enough. For XP to work you need to think about how the team interacts as a group and works as individuals.

Setting up an environment where a team can work is the most important, but often the most easily ignored, part of a project. Your physical setup is important because the better the environment the happier and more productive your team and the better the end product. There are three important factors to consider in the way the development environment is organized:

✧ The work space

✧ The location of the customer

✧ The timing of the work

The Work Space

It is hard to do XP in traditional cubicles and offices. Instead, the team should be clustered together. In most places we have worked, there is an area for programmers, another for graphic designers, and still another for project managers. This setup impedes pairing from different departments and can often lead to warring groups unwilling to share responsibility.

Seating Arrangements

It is much more productive to place people together randomly, with the project manager sitting beside a programmer or a programmer beside a graphic designer and a copywriter. If at all possible, put junior people close to senior people. If you can, try to provide a nonworking space for people's belongings. When you do this you break down attachments to workstations and people end up working close to those they are interacting with, breaking and forming attachments as needed. Desk attachment is hard to overcome, but when you succeed the whole process of pairing becomes organic.

Desks and Chairs

Give everyone big surfaces. We would rather have someone at a big $40 folding table than at a small $400 desk. There should be room to spread out cards and sketches. Everyone should have enough space to host a second person at her station.

Invest in good chairs for workstations that provide ample support for the back. You get much better work out of people when they can function in comfort. In our company all the furniture combined cost less than one of our chairs. Be sure that the chairs you pick are adjustable to fit the needs of different-sized people and that they can easily roll from one desk to another. If you do it right, people will become more territorial about their chair than about the desk they are working at.

Hardware and Platforms

After chairs, if you splurge anywhere, do it on big monitors and good computers. Web development uses a lot of software at the same time, and most of it has substantial RAM and processing requirements. Browsers and IDEs are pigs and will crawl if not given tremendous power. Many developers will want to see a browser and their development tool, be it Photoshop or Visual Studio, at the same time. Big monitors also make working in tandem easier.

Get your graphic designers off Macintoshes! We are big Mac fans and have a great deal of respect for the operating system (OS), but it is a fact of life that most Web team use Windows. Furthermore, Macs are brighter than PCs. So many times we have seen a design created and shown to the customer on a Mac and then found that it was too dark for the general audience, which is 95 percent Windows users. It pains us to say it, but every Web development tool that we have ever seen is either not available for Mac or has a perfectly good equivalent on Windows. Photoshop and Illustrator are identical on both platforms. The only role with an argument for having a Mac is the tester and then only if the customer has selected to support the platform.

A Shared Repository

Once everyone is working on the same platform, you should make an image of a clean install of the OS and all of the applications that anyone on the team uses. Doing this allows you to install a fresh computing environment for everyone when software changes or when a computer is having a problem. With all files in a shared repository, it is possible for a developer to sit at any station to do her work.

Discussion Spaces

Buy several round tables and place them out of earshot of the development environment. Often groups of three or more will need a place to go off and collaborate on a problem. If you don't establish these areas, noise will become a problem. Use your worst chairs in these quiet areas. It should never be comfortable to sit in a meeting all day.

Walls

Walls are for writing on. Every piece of wall should be available for posting status information, stories, and designs. Everyone should be able to draw a design on the wall to illustrate a point. In some places the walls are covered with a whiteboard wallpaper so the team can draw and erase anywhere.

Food

Snacks should be readily available, and food should be brought in regularly. Some people see this as extravagant, but it is actually very cost effective. One developer walking to a store to get a bottle of water costs more than providing water for the entire team for a week. Chips, pop, water, cookies, and crunchy vegetables should be restocked weekly. Give the project manager a budget. We bet you can keep the larder full for less than the price of one billable hour a week. If the team is working through a meal, bring one in for them. Don't make this a practice, though. Lunch breaks are an important rest from the project that everyone needs.

Locating the Customer

Onsite customers are beneficial, but it is possible to have too much of a good thing. The customer is a member of the team, but it is frankly a little creepy to find yourself, as a junior graphic designer, permanently sitting beside the person who writes the checks. We want the customer to get an even view of the project and, when put in with the team, she should start to see things through the eyes of the people she has the most contact with rather than the team as a whole.

The customer should be given a desk away from the team. She is welcome to sit at anyone's workstation, and you should make sure that everyone else on the team is clear about that. However, she should have her own place to call home. She will appreciate this, especially if you give her a phone and some privacy. Often the customer has a job to do outside of the project, and the easier you make it for her to do that job from your location, the better. Talk to the customer's IT department; maybe you can get her on her company's VPN so she can use files and be connected to its calendar and mail.

Work Timing

The work environment is set up to help the team get the most out of every hour, not to sequester them. XP introduces the concept of "velocity," which includes setting a sustainable pace for a project. Web projects sorely need this.

Avoiding Burnout

When you do your first Web site and work four months straight twelve hours a day, it can be justifiably considered a right of passage. If you are still doing this by your fourth Web site, it has become bad project management and speaks to nonexistent customer expectation management. If this is how your company works, get out before you burn out. Every project will have instances where people have to work long hours, but these should be rare occasions with darn good reasons.

Setting Velocity

As stated in Chapter 4, we set our velocity in the release plan at the start of the project. We select the number of people on the team and multiply it by 50 billable working hours for a two-week iteration. Every week we expect our team to put in 5 hours each day working on the project undistracted, including attending meetings. Teams will differ in how much you can ask of them, but be clear about your expectations and be flexible in how different people meet them. Some team members will do 10 hours one week and 40 the next. Others will consistently do 25 hours each week. Make your judgments over a longer scale.

Time Tracking

Automate your time tracking system. As the project manager you must account to the customer for the time spent on a project. Time sheets handed in weekly are difficult to maintain, so if you can't track time via an automated system, get the numbers for the past day at each morning's standup meeting. You should be putting this information into a spreadsheet or other system so you can keep a journal of estimates against actuals. The team needs constant feedback about their estimates if improvements are to occur.

Breaking the XP Rules

Use all of the advice just given as a guideline. We have tried setting up the perfect XP lab, and the team used it far differently from what we had expected. We built a pair programming area with two huge monitors on each table, but each day the team was still working in pairs at their desks. We would have done a better job by just giving each person one of the huge monitors and forgetting our fancy lab.

As the XP coach of your team, your job is to get them to try new things and learn from what works. To do this you will force some practices on them that they will chafe under, but you need them to experiment. Don't force too much change on them too fast unless they are receptive. In the end go with what works—you won't be forced to turn in your XP membership card if you break a few XP rules.

Chapter 7

Working in Iterations

Web projects are traditionally done in waterfall style with define, design, develop, and deploy stages each taking months. These projects can be done more effectively and with less risk following short iterations of a couple of weeks.

An iteration formally starts when the customer signs an iteration plan. This document is both a schedule of the iteration and a detailed description of the deliverables, including the acceptance criteria that the deliverables need to achieve. The plan should not be long or overly detailed. The customer reviews and signs it prior to the beginning of any work.

Successful projects are determined in the first three to five iterations. These iterations are where we need to achieve the following goals:

- Set up the development environment
- Get the team working as a single productive unit
- Get the customer comfortable with the XP process
- Explore the major risks of the project

The largest fundamental difference between software projects and Web projects is that in Web projects there is a distinct order of operations. To see how this affects Web XP projects and the iterative process, we need to take a closer look at

- ✧ Stories and deliverables

- ✧ The iteration strategy session

- ✧ Iteration planning and estimating

- ✧ Iteration 1: preparing for development

- ✧ Iteration 2: avoiding risk

- ✧ Iteration 3: spikes

- ✧ The iterations ahead

Stories and Deliverables

One of the better attributes of XP is expressing work to be done in "stories." A story represents an idea for a feature. In pure XP stories come from the customer, but in Web projects we have to break this rule. Customers may have an easy time of writing stories for functions that they can relate to in their work experience, like "Check that the selected product is in stock," but they often have problems with others.

When we first started using XP for our Web projects, we tried stories like "Create a Products page" or "Create an About Us section." These stories never worked because they were too large. Even the smallest page in a Web project assumes that you have an approved design and copy and images for it. Our stories changed quickly to "Collect content for an About Us page," "Select images for Products pages," and a myriad of others for the graphic design process.[1]

---

1. Chapter 8 discusses the graphic design process in detail.

Here we run smack into a contradiction between traditional XP and XP for Web projects. Stories should be connected to a direct business value, but some of our stories are tasks and it is hard to make a clear connection to the business value they provide. Nonetheless, XP has to be bent for the parts of Web projects that are more for presentation than for functionality. If not, your team will be blocked. This is a call that needs to be made by the project manager. In Web projects stories must demonstrate business or project value.

One of the problems related to Web projects is that the customer is rarely aware of the need for a distinct order of operations; this can affect the presentation of deliverables. In Part III we explore design patterns in Web projects that allow us to deconstruct Web pages so that we can have tangible deliverables for parts of those pages. Parts can be made into individual stories that are demonstratable, but Web projects still need an experienced project manager and development team to set the order of operations for when stories should be completed.

This isn't to say that the customer is out of the loop. We start each iteration with an iteration strategy session led by the strategist or project manager.

The Iteration Strategy Session

This meeting includes the customer, the strategist, the project manager, and the design and technical leads. In it we review progress made against the release plan and write stories. The project manager is the primary source of stories in the first five iterations. The tasks done in these early stages are common to most Web projects, so our estimates are better than average.

The purpose of iteration strategy is to assess the business objectives of the customer and to organize future development to best meet them. The strategy session focuses on four main areas: writing stories, estimating stories, the metrics of success, and selecting stories.

Review the Release Plan at each iteration to see
how the project is doing and if the plan
still reflects the customer's needs.

Writing Stories

The strategist, the project manager, or the customer comes to the meeting with stories written; alternatively we write them on the spot. Often we write the stories for the first few iterations so that the customer can see the thought process behind them.

Estimating Stories

Once we have stories, the strategy team gives gross estimates, which are in days. Forget about hours; talking about hours is too fine a level of detail for estimating. The smallest increment should be a half day.

Success Metrics

The stories described may function as stated, but that doesn't guarantee business success. Each story or group of stories has associated success metrics that state how we calculate the success or failure of a development effort. Are we looking to generate traffic, increase revenue, change patterns of behavior, or save money? Once we determine the kind of success we are looking for, we quantify this and plan how we will track our results. These tracking methods often end up generating new stories.

Selecting Stories

Once we have estimates, the customer can prioritize the stories and select which ones are to be done in an iteration. Should the customer need to increase the number of stories to more than the iteration will allow, the project manager can, in some cases, enlarge the development team prior to the planning session.

In the first few iterations, the stories are dictated by the order of operations in the graphic design process, the environment setup, and other constraints on the Web development process.

Iteration Planning and Estimating

Planning with the customer is an important part of the process. In XP we expect our team to take responsibility for estimates, so we give them the right to make their own. The iteration planning session includes everyone from development and focuses on five key topics.

Discussing Stories

Here the customer reads the stories to the team and the team asks questions about them. Short stories are expanded to describe in detail what is to be created.

Assigning Stories

Stories are championed by team members. Every story has a champion who is primarily responsible for its completion.

Revising Estimates

Developers revise the estimate of time to complete the story if necessary. It is never a bad thing to tell the project manager or strategist that her gross estimate was off. You just have to say why.

Determining Content Requirements

All required content from the customer is itemized, and strategies to get the content are agreed on. This is an opportunity for the customer to back out of a story that may have too high a demand on his time.

Risk Analysis and Management

What will cause our estimates to fail? This is an opportunity to look at risks associated with stories. Are we using an unproven technology? Are we relying on a third party for content? Here we look at the potential risks and jointly decide what to do if the worst does happen.

In the next sections we lay out the first few iterations of a Web project. If you are familiar with XP, you will quickly see that our approach is far more constrained than what XP proposes. This is for two reasons. First, teams that have never done XP will likely find this guide smoothing their transition by ensuring that at the end of iteration 3, they have a good foundation across graphic design and functionality. Second, Web sites are not object oriented. In Part III we will see how to impose a pseudo-object model on Web pages. These iterations are constrained to accommodate this structure. More than rules, they are themes about how to get started and how to minimize risks.

Iteration 1: Preparing for Development

In the first iteration strategy session, the customer is just a bystander; the technical lead presents the stories to set up the development environment. We used to call this iteration 0, but it ruined the numbering system. Now we call it iteration 1, although it is spiritually a zero iteration. Here we do no programming and only explore the beginnings of the design process. Iteration 1 is about the development server setup, revision control, the build manager, and other stories focused on preparing for development.

We have worked on projects where this was not done up front, causing needless risk. Don't wait until code is scattered across ten computers to get it into a repository. Don't wait until iteration 5 to install the database. In the first iteration all the software needed for the project should be integrated. Find out now that the application server you have selected will not accept your database driver. After iteration 1 any member of the team should be able to do her work, check it in, build it, run it, and move it to QA when it is ready for release.

Write tests to prove that everything is working. Most projects will have a developer IDE, a revision control system, a build manager system, an HTTP server, an application server, and a database. Script a checkin of simple code that puts the words "Hello World" into the database and a unit test to display it in a Web browser.[2] This test will prove that the stories from the iteration were done and will help to determine that your system is functioning correctly. It is quite common in Web projects to hunt for a bug in code for days, only to find that the registry has eaten a DLL that makes your database work. In many Web projects a majority of the functionality is centered on writing to and reading from a database, so the tests you create in iteration 1 are the foundation for most of the tests you are going to write in the future.

---

2. See Chapter 14 for a full discussion of unit testing.

Iteration 1 has set the stage to get some work done, but at the same time you have taken the customer though a complete iteration with stories, acceptance tests, standup meetings, and paired development. Up to now the customer has had little to contribute but has been able to watch. Trust us, in the first iteration most customers are too overwhelmed by watching and asking questions to contribute much. What is most important is that this first iteration stands a good chance of success. Succeeding at this point is your most important goal because you have given your team confidence and earned needed customer trust. On more than one occasion, we have heard the customer say, "Hey, you guys really do know what you're doing!"

Here are some obligatory stories from a typical first iteration:

- Design questions
- Competitive analysis
- Mood board
- Development server—install and configure OS
- Development server—install and configure browsers
- Development server—install and configure ISAPI filter
- Development server—install and configure database
- Development server—install and configure database XML tools
- Development server—install and configure revision control software
- Development server—install and configure Web server
- Create image of development server and backup
- Run mirror on testing server
- Run mirror on customer preview server

Iteration 2: Avoiding Risk

With a successful first iteration, you can get some work done. But take it easy—you still have a new customer and perhaps a team that is not used to working together or with XP. Do easy stories in this iteration to get another success under your belt. Learn how the team works together and how well they estimate and improve their estimates each day. Give extra time to writing acceptance tests. Focus on getting started on the graphic design stories and some straightforward functional stories. Let the customer pick a fun functional story. Stay away from risk in this iteration—working with a new team is risky enough.

The following stories implement *sitemap.xml,* your Web site. It may not be what your client had in mind for a release, but in theory it is complete and functional. In iteration 1 you set up the server, so now you are at a place four weeks into the project that waterfall Web

The first few iterations are about finding project "risks"; deal with risks early or you may fall though the ice too far from shore.

projects won't reach for two to three more months. In waterfall projects the customer gets nothing until he gets everything. As an illustration, here are some obligatory stories from a typical second iteration:

- Design candidates
- Create *sitemap.xml* and run site structure script
- Content catalog of what is available for the project
- Content collection—"Who We Are"
- Content collection—"What We Do"

Iteration 3: Spikes

Welcome to your first high-risk iteration. Some of the best advice passed on to us was to do the easiest thing first and then the hardest. Iterations 1 and 2 broke in the team and hopefully worked out any kinks. Now we want to explore the risks of the project that pertain to technical difficulty and feasibility.

Iterative development is first about reducing the risks of complex projects. Moving risk to the beginning of the project allows the team to find out early if something can't be done as planned or if it should reexamine the Release Plan.

In iteration 3 we need to do a lot of what are called "spikes," or proofs of concept. We isolate the hardest, riskiest parts of the project and write enough tests and code to see that we can do it and to see what doing it entails. Can you get an important JavaScript function to work in all of the browsers you need to support? Can your server-side application dump a file into the company's legacy system? If you haven't done something before, add a spike for it.

The design department can also do spikes, given the number of graphic design ideas that are tricky or impossible to do in a browser. In one of our recent projects, we wanted to put an animated menu on an angle without using Flash. We did a spike to see if it could be done in DHTML. It couldn't, so we had to change the plan to add stories for creating a different design for non-Flash users.

At the end of iteration 3, leave time to update the release plan with the customer. You will be surprised how easygoing the customer is about changes when a launch date isn't just around the corner. We have never encountered a problem that couldn't be resolved if found early in a project.

Here are some obligatory stories from a typical third iteration:

✧ Color palette

✧ CSS—home page

✧ CSS—inside pages

✧ Page layout—XSL for home page

✧ Page layout—XSL for template portions of inside pages

✧ Wire frames—"Keyword Search" section

✧ XML modeling—"FAQs"

✧ Content collection—"Our Partners"

✧ Content collection—"Our Experience"

✧ Content programming—"Who We Are"

✧ Content programming—"What We Do"

The Iterations Ahead

By now you have revamped the release plan into a far more realistic projection, your team is working in a stable and predicable environment, your customer understands the XP process and her role in it, and you have some successes to feel good about. We have outlined these as the first three iterations, but think of them more as three themes to go through. On some projects setup will take two or even three iterations. You may need a few to get the customer up to speed or to get the team working well in XP. Iterations 1 through 3 for another team may be iterations 1 through 6 for yours. All projects are different. In any event you will notice that the role of the strategist is reduced by this time and that the customer has begun to be of more assistance in writing stories.

In future iterations you will find that you have achieved a sustainable velocity and that your estimates are getting better. The challenge in selecting stories now is in balancing them between design, server-side functions, and client-side functions. Though these are explicitly interdependent in the first few iterations, you will want to move ahead in parallel to use the team evenly and progress the site. The following are a number of obligatory stories for subsequent iterations. To these, as to the earlier iteration stories, you will need to add spikes and other functional and content-related stories that are unique to your project.

Typical Iteration 4 stories include

- Content collection—"Careers"
- Content collection—"Products"
- Content programming—"Our Partners"
- Content programming—"Our Experience"
- Content layout—"Who We Are"
- Content layout—"What We Do"
- Import content—"FAQs"

Typical Iteration 5 stories include

- Content layout—"Our Partners"
- Content layout—"Our Experience"
- Content layout—"FAQs"

- ✧ Content programming—"Careers"

- ✧ Import content—"Products"

You now see how the XP iterative process can be applied to a Web development project. Throughout all of the iterations the graphic design process is also ongoing. In the next chapter we explore how this process is affected by XP principles.

Chapter 8

The Graphic Design Process

*One picture is worth more than
a thousand words.*
—Chinese Proverb

*Practices and documents that help the customer make small
incremental decisions are a focus of XP and the foundation of
our XP'd graphic design process.*

XP allows the customer to make decisions and set priorities. In
Web XP this principle applies to the graphic design process as much
as to other parts of a project. In fact, one of the reasons that XP
attracted us was its emphasis on customer involvement because, in
our experience, the more the customer is involved in the design process the happier she is with the results and the more she trusts the
designer.

The Pitfalls of Ignoring the Customer during Design

Sometimes designers rely too much on their own expertise and ignore the customer as a valuable resource. Too often designers meet the customer for only one day and present a design the following week. Sometimes designs are even presented to prospective customers in order to win a pitch. None of this sufficiently involves the customer.

Why is it wrong to just leap in and start designing? First, the requirements are completely subjective. We can't tell you the number of times we have heard a customer tell us he wanted a design to be "corporate and clean" or "fun, very hip, and easy to use." What that means to the customer often means something completely different to the designer. The question at this point isn't "Are we ready to design?" It's "What does 'clean' mean?" Language is useless in design because any requirement can be interpreted differently by different people.

Second, designing without customer involvement misses out on a valuable opportunity to build customer trust. How do you develop that trust? Simply involve the customer in the design process.

Graphic Design Iterations

Develop stories that can be achieved over several iterations with deliverables for the customer to approve. Here are some recommendations that will help give the designer and customer a better understanding of the brand and how to bring it online:

- ✧ Creative brief
- ✧ Competitive analysis
- ✧ Mood board

- Look-and-feel candidates
- Design specification
- Page layout

The Creative Brief

The first step in any creative process is to get an idea of the corporate brand. This requires a review of the company's logo and branding documents and any marketing and communications materials. Some companies have already gone through the process of defining their brand and have detailed documents showing how their logo can be used. This is extremely helpful, but unfortunately such material is not always available. Many times, the customer has problems providing a copy of the logo in digital format. One customer handed us a Swiss Army knife with its logo and said, "This is my brand."

Over the years we have come up with a standard set of questions to define a corporate brand as it exists today and in the future and what it is meant to convey. The creative brief is a summary of this information. It is vital in setting the constraints of any design that will be undertaken and varies in severity from customer to customer.

The Competitive Analysis

With an initial idea of the corporate brand, we still need to define where the customer fits in the marketplace—that is, who else is competing for the attention of the target audience. After a review of up to thirty Web sites, we pull out between five and ten that illustrate some of our findings. This sample illustrates trends in colors, navigation, content, and functionality.

For each of these five to ten Web sites, we identify what was done successfully and what was done poorly. This sets out some of the possibilities for our project. It also helps customers communicate what they like and don't like in the context of their own industry and about sites in general. For example, we get a chance to hear that they don't like dark sites or sites that have small text or menus with icons instead of text.

The Mood Board

With two stories successfully completed, your customer is beginning trust you and feel as though she has a real say on the site's appearance. But you are not yet ready to make the giant leap to design. After all, you still have to interpret the brand from words to images. Not only is a picture is worth a thousand words—it is also worth a thousand man hours of rebuilding lost customer trust, so don't take any unnecessary risks.

The next story is all about pictures, because a brand is really all about creating a mood or an impression. That is why we develop a mood board. A *mood board* is a large piece of cardboard covered in cuttings from magazines. It is a collage of everything that you have learned so far in the form of images, colors, fonts, textures, shapes, photography, and illustrations and their various combinations.

The mood board is a good way to narrow down the design possibilities.

The cornerstone of our design methodology, a mood board is where the designer can represent different graphical concepts and group clippings into a "safe" mood or perhaps a "risky" mood. During the presentation of the mood board to the customer, expect to make pages of notes on what the customer meant by "conservative" or "hip."

While the mood board takes only a day to put together, it saves weeks in miscommunication. We have worked with designers who skipped this step on small-budget projects, thinking it would save some time. Think again. No matter how well you think you know the customer's brand, you don't. You can't possibly until you have illustrated some creative features. And what takes longer to generate: a Web site design or a mood board? Since each design can take 20 to 30 hours and a mood board takes approximately 5 hours, which step would you rather have to redo? Also, we have never had to redo a mood board or a design when we have followed this process.

Look and Feel

At this point we have refined the definition of what the customer is looking for. We have narrowed down the infinite possibilities to some clear constraints. With the mood board in hand, we develop three distinct designs based on feedback from the customer. Each design consists of

- A home page at 800 by 600 and 1,024 by 769 pixels
- An inside page at 800 by 600 and 1,024 by 769 pixels
- A color palette
- A list of fonts

The two design resolutions help to show how each design will stretch or shrink to fit the user's monitor, which not only helps the customer visualize the design but also shows how the interface programmer plans to map out the page.

Mockups of a home page and an inside page are created
based on ideas gleaned from the mood board.

Presenting these designs is very low stress. Because the customer
has been involved in all of the meetings, he isn't surprised by what
he sees and is ready for what he is being shown. He has arrived there
in small progressive steps, making decisions all the way through.

The customer can choose from a number
of designs, usually three.

The Design Specification

The customer has by now selected one of the design candidates,
but there is always some tweaking to be done. With changes we also
deliver a clearer definition of the site's style in the form of a Cascading Style Sheet (CSS), which is developed by the designer with help
from the interface programmer. The CSS defines the colors, fonts,
and other attributes for each element required in the design.

The Page Layout

With the home page and inside templates approved, the interface programmer and designer work their way through the site, programming the layout for each page. The content is placed on the page, the layout is applied, the customer approves the layout, and on we go to the next page.

Matching Tasks and Iterations

We recommend that the design process be done over three, two-week iterations. In the first iteration you can complete the creative brief and the competitive analysis. In the second iteration you can easily complete the mood board. In the third iteration you spend the entire time on producing and presenting the design candidates. In the fourth iteration you complete the design specifications and program the home page XSLT and the main inside page XSLT. In the fifth iteration you begin the page layout.

Part III

XML and Web XP

XP requires the team to have the courage to make changes to code at any time and anywhere. Refactoring and continuous integration rely on a framework of object-oriented programming and an arsenal of unit tests. This is fine for the server-side programming elements of Web projects, but what about pages?

Pages are not objects. They are brittle and difficult to manage and unit tests can't tell you that an important sentence is missing or that the wrong image is being displayed.

Part III looks at how XML works in XP Web development. We start with a discussion of HTML and its limitations in Web site design. Then we turn to basic XML and its obvious advantages. Finally we look at how XML works in actual XP Web development practice.

Chapter 9

XML—A Better Way

With HTML we build brittle, unmaintainable sites. XML frees us to create fluid site architectures that are change friendly and easy to maintain. Pages are not objects yet, but we are getting close.

XML is an important development in Web technology that has been around for a few years now. Sometime over the last two or three years however, advancement in the standards process and availability of tools have made it extremely usable in today's Web development environment. Still while the buzz about XML is everywhere and XML use is increasing, there are still a huge number of people and companies who don't use it efficiently for everyday Web development.

XML offers many benefits to all developers, whether or not they are using XP. However, some of XML's features support XP in a highly synergistic way. A complete explanation of XML is beyond the scope of this book, but we will quickly run down some of its advantages in XP development. After that, in Chapter 10 we will introduce a specific Web site design architecture that takes advantage of many XML and XSLT features.

Before we start, let's review existing Web development practices so we can see what problems XML helps fix.

HTML

The backend infrastructure of most Web sites today is a hodge-podge of code in a number of languages. Typically there are static HTML files, graphic images, dynamic scripted templates, DHTML scripts for client-side interactivity, business objects, databases, legacy systems, middleware adapters, and content management systems—all thrown together to form a collection of interlinked Web pages.

In any Web system most of these pages usually have a number of common elements: content, navigation components, and graphic

When you build Web sites in HTML, you risk an eternity
of "painful" code maintenance.

design (branding). Across multiple pages of a single Web site, there is usually a somewhat uniform application of design elements. Navigation and page layout are uniformly structured from page to page and section to section, but the actual menu choices tend to change depending on your current location. Content changes from page to page, and often a dynamically generated page will be different every time it is loaded.

This dynamism is usually produced by scripting templates, written in any number of programming languages and environments such as JSP, ASP, PHP, and Cold Fusion. With a traditional Web architecture, these scripts call on objects in the business logic tier to retrieve content (from files, content management systems, legacy system middleware adapters, or databases). Once they have retrieved the data to be presented, they format it for display in a Web page by churning through it and wrapping HTML tags around the various fields. This is an effective process that has worked well for a number of years. Nevertheless, it is not without its drawbacks.

HTML Problems

The first problem with the approach just described is that a programming language such as Java, VB, or Perl is used to specify formatting, design, and layout. This means that programmers who aren't good at or interested in graphic design spend a lot of time on frustrating and annoying details of HTML page layout. It also means that visual-design–oriented developers who don't consider themselves hardcore programmers need to learn a scripting language (or several if they want to develop in more than one environment) and muck around with data access and intermediary APIs. A number of talented developers manage to enjoy and excel at both application programming and graphic design, but they are few and far between.

For programmers the issue isn't that page layout in HTML is *hard*; it is that it is time-consuming work focused on visual details that most programmers couldn't care less about. For them, nothing is more frustrating and disheartening than completing an important piece of functionality with an elegant, scalable, robust, and flawlessly working code structure, only to have some nitwit from the customer's marketing department return with a five-page list of "bugs" such as "Subsection heading font too small," "Buttons should be aligned with right edge of paragraph," "Table columns in wrong order," and the dreaded "Page looks too cluttered." Not only is the work tedious and dull but it also represents time that a highly paid programmer could spend on more complex and important tasks.

These problems are exacerbated when it is time for a visual redesign of a site. If all of the HTML formatting is intermingled with programming code in many different modules, it becomes a daunting task to make the necessary changes. Usually it is possible to do this only by bringing programmers back into the project because they are the only ones who can decipher the code.

Yet another problem is that effective automated unit testing is at best limited on HTML pages. The final output of a JSP script is essentially a long string, which in a browser is parsed into tags, text, links, and scripts. But outside of the browser, you need an HTML parser to look inside the string to verify the contents of the Web page. Generically parsing Web pages is tricky because many contain sloppy HTML and errors such as improperly nested tags. Many browsers do the best they can with bad HTML and usually display something on the screen, albeit in sometimes unpredictable ways.

HTTPUnit

HTTPUnit does a decent job of addressing the testing problem. However, the API gives you only limited functionality to test tables and forms, providing no advanced testing of the page structure and layout. You can use HTTPUnit to convert a Web page into XHTML (an XML-compliant variation of HTML) and process it as an XML document, but in order to do that HTTPUnit must run your original page through JTidy.

JTidy is a Java version of Tidy, a module that cleans up messy HTML and optionally outputs XHTML.[1] It often makes guesses as to what was meant when moderate HTML problems are encountered, and it does as good a job as can be expected under such circumstances. Tidy is a great thing to have when you need it, but the bottom line is that it changes your original document, so that tests you execute on the cleaned-up XHMTL do not actually reflect the original document. This could have the unwanted effect of hiding errors from your test script. And, besides, if you are going to use an XML parser for unit testing on your final HTML output, why not simply create your final output as XHTML in the first place? We will show how much more efficiently all this can be done with XML and XSLT.

A corollary to this is the fact that HTML Web pages contain a mess of tags, text, and script code. This often makes it difficult to locate various page elements in the source code. Writing scripted

HTML Web sites are tangled messes
of interfaces, content, and code.

1. See *http://tidy.sourceforge.net/* for more information on Tidy.

unit tests to make sure that various elements in a design-rich page are present, in the right place, laid out properly, and contain the right content is not at all easy. There is simply no practical, standard, programmatic way to do it.

XML to the Rescue

Before we get into a detailed discussion of how to use XML, we should introduce some of its basic concepts and technologies. This should provide enough background for you to understand the advantages of incorporating XML technology into XP Web development projects.

Basic XML

XML is a markup language similar to HTML. An XML document is simply a text file containing a hierarchical collection of *nodes*, such as elements, attributes, processing instructions, and text. An important property of XML is its support of semantic rather than formatting markup. Unlike HTML, which uses a set of pre-defined tags, XML gives developers the freedom to mark up their content semantically and to make their own tags. For example, a product can be represented using tags such as `<product>`, `<code>`, `<price>`, `<size>`, and `<description>`.

Parsers

One of the cornerstones of XML is its use of parsers to read XML files and identify the XML nodes within. A number of XML parsers are available in many different programming environments. All of them present an API to read or write to the nodes in an XML document. Without a parser, an XML document is nothing but a text string that is difficult to process or modify.

Validation

An important function of XML parsers is document validation—that is, checking an XML document for conformance with a schema document or DTD. The base XML specification defines the concept of a *validating parser*. This is simply a generic XML parser that is capable of validating any XML document given the appropriate schema. The parser reads the XML file and the schema document and generates an error if any of the rules specified in the schema are violated.

Schemas

The schema document defines the valid structure of the XML content. Schemas allow you to specify the element names allowed in a document, the attributes allowed in each element, and the way elements can be nested. They also allow you to specify certain data types for attributes and text nodes.

Validation is a simple concept but a very powerful one. For XP projects XML validation adds a new technique to the unit testing toolkit.

Schemas versus DTDs

Schemas and DTDs are two ways to specify the structure of an XML document. DTDs are an older standard and come out of XML's SGML roots. Schemas are more recent and much more sophisticated. Unlike DTDs, schema documents are themselves well-formed XML and can be read with an XML parser. It is preferable to work with schemas rather than DTDs for XML validation, however, everything in this chapter applies equally well to both.

XSLT

Once you have marked up your content in XML, you need a way to specify how it is to be formatted and displayed on a Web page. This is where XSLT comes in.

XSLT, a sister technology to XML, is a transformation language designed to translate XML documents from one format to another. You can use it to output any kind of formatted text. Depending on how you write them, XSLT templates can output flat text files, CSV files, HTML, XHTML, or any kind of XML. For Web development the common approach is to use XSLT to transform semantically marked up XML page content into display-formatted HTML or XHTML Web pages.

XSLT processors are for many platforms that conform to W3C standards, including Java (Xalan) and Microsoft (MSXML), which means that XSLT style sheets are portable.

Learning XSLT

Some developers find XSLT difficult to work with at first. This is likely because it is a declarative, rule-based language rather than a procedural or object-oriented one. Learning XSLT requires you to leave behind a number of familiar programming concepts and to start thinking in terms of transformations, match patterns, namespaces, node sets, result tree fragments, and the like. It has often been said that years of programming procedurally can be an obstacle to learning object-oriented programming, and we think the same can be said for learning XSLT. Still, our experience is that, once mastered, XSLT is a powerful, intuitive, flexible, and elegant language to work in.

Client-Side XSLT

In a Web environment you have the choice of performing the XSLT transformation on the client or on the server. Web browsers such as Internet Explorer 6.0 and Netscape Navigator 6 ship with fully W3C-compliant XSLT processors. In an intranet environment or administrative backend to a public Web site, where you can require users to install level-6 browsers, you can develop entire Web applications that send nothing but XML to the browser and have all of the XSLT transformations done on the client side. For public Web sites you can have your server check for the browser version number in the HTTP request header and do the XSLT transformation server side only for non-XSLT–compliant browsers.

As time progresses and more and more people migrate to level-6 and higher browsers, Web servers will be increasingly able to offload XSLT processing to the client, thereby greatly enhancing the scalability of XML-based Web sites.

Chapter 10

XP Web Development Practices

Separating content, design, and functionality from each other is a major theme in software development. Finally XML allows us to do the same with Web pages.

On Web projects our goal is to separate how a page looks, what content it contains, and what functions it performs into independent entities. HTML is the total antithesis to this approach. Enter XML. In this chapter we present a framework of how XML and XSLT can be used to create flexible Web sites.

XML in Web Development

Let's look at some of the implications of using XML and XSLT in Web site development, so we can see what advantages they offer to the team. What we mean is developing the site in such a way that every page is encoded as XML before it is transformed for display into

HTML by an XSLT style sheet. This is a very important design decision that requires the development team to follow some strict rules.

The First Law of XML Web Development

The first and most fundamental rule is that no formatted HTML code should be generated anywhere other than in the XSLT style sheets. We call this the first law of XML Web development, and it means that static content stored on the file system should be encoded as XML rather than HTML. It also means that any programming code that retrieves data from databases or business objects for display on a Web page should always mark up that data using semantically meaningful XML tags rather than formatted HTML. The XML is concise and direct: As we said earlier, tags mark up content semantically with tag names that are similar or identical to names of objects, properties, tables, and columns used by the program.

Using the Schema Document

The content of various pages and sections of a site will have different XML structures. It is important to decide on the exact nature of those structures, which can be formalized by a schema document. A single Web site may use different schemas for different content sections of a page. Most sites will contain some generic copy for which a schema using familiar HTML-like paragraph and heading tags may be appropriate. An e-commerce site will have pages that contain product descriptions, requiring a schema with element and attribute names like "product," "description," "price," and "size," and an order placement system that makes use of XML node names such as "shopping cart," "quantity," and "shipping address." One way of managing this is to specify the structure of each content type using separate subschemas and then creating a "master" schema that references these subschemas.

There are many efforts under way to standardize DTDs and schemas for specific industries and business domains, and it always makes sense to look for a standard schema or DTD that fits your needs before you write your own, even if your current requirements are only for internal use. Doing this could very well lay the groundwork for future interoperability of your system with others.

One important function of a schema is as a contractual agreement between the various producers and users of XML. This is true in much the same sense that an application programming interface (API) is often a contractual agreement between developers of classes and developers using those classes. For businesses exchanging purchase orders encoded in XML messages, this agreement ensures interoperability of the systems involved. For a small Web team consisting of programmers, content managers, and style sheet designers, this agreement ensures that the XSLT templates created by the designers will work properly with the content and the dynamic data.

Using the XSLT Style Sheet

Once the first law of XML development has been accepted as a development practice, responsibility for all of the "look-and-feel" formatting of the site rests in a single location, the XSLT style sheet. With it designers become free to work on the design of the site unfettered by programming concerns. They can specialize in XSLT and HTML and do not need to learn a plethora of APIs and general-purpose programming and scripting languages because their XSLT skills are portable from one environment to the next. At the same time programmers are relieved of the burden of responsibility to graphic designers.

Separating Content and Formatting

By encoding all content as XML, you completely separate content from formatting. This is in keeping with the classic n-tier software architectural principle of separating presentation from business logic and data access. In fact, this approach can be described simply as implementing the presentation tier in XSL and using XML as an interface between it and the business/application logic tier.

The fact is that there is *nothing* you can do in XML/XSLT that you can't do with programming code. What XSL adds is tremendous simplicity and elegance. In addition to the important advantage of separate responsibilities for programming and design, there are numerous other ways in which this separation of content from formatting benefits a Web development team.

Code Reuse

By marking up page content with a semantically meaningful XML structure, you open up new possibilities for code reuse. To illustrate this, let's look at a Web page that displays international currencies and their current exchange rates relative to some base currency. The page is built dynamically with JSP by querying an object that has access to a periodically updated currency feed. Rather than having the JSP return an HTML page with the currencies laid out in a table, we code the JSP to output an XML file that looks like this:

```
<exchange_rates base="USD">
    <currency symbol="EUR">
        <name>Euro</name>
        <rate>0.8532</rate>
    </currency>
    <currency symbol="CAD">
        <name>Canadian Dollar</name>
        <rate>0.6492</rate>
    </currency>
    <currency symbol="USD">
        <name>United States Dollar</name>
        <rate>1.0000</rate>
    </currency>
    …more currencies here
</ exchange_rates>
```

You can do many different things with this. You can create an XSLT style sheet to display a list of exchange rates as an HTML table. You can then create a new set of XSLT templates to produce a DHTML currency calculator. Or you can create a whole new set of style sheets to format the rate table and calculator using WebML for display in a Wireless Application Protocol (WAP) browser. All of this can be done without ever touching the original JSP.

You can also make the currency table available as a Web service. Remote customer applications can retrieve the raw XML from the server and parse the data for internal use. With a little bit of work, you can even add some functionality to support SOAP-formatted requests and responses, outputting the same XML structure inside a SOAP wrapper.

Redesigning a Site

A related advantage of separating content from formatting reveals itself when it is time for a graphic design overhaul of the site. All of the design code resides in a set of XSLT files located conveniently in one place, which greatly simplifies the redesign process. Compare this to a traditional Web architecture, where HTML formatting code is scattered around and embedded in a jumble of script code and HTML files.

Asynchronous Development

An unexpected effect of design/content separation of is the ability to support asynchronous development. That is, programmers and style sheet designers can work on their areas without being affected by each other's progress. Asynchronicity can be easily accomplished by the use of dummy XML files, with which you can create output templates for dynamic pages before the dynamic functionality is completed.

Let's take a basic shopping cart application, in which a shopping cart and its contents can be represented by an XML file.

```
        <page name="shopping_cart_view">
Cocoon   <title>Your Shopping Cart</title>
        <content>
            <shopping_cart>
                <item code="53942">
                    <description>"radical" wool knit sweater
                        </description>
                    <qantity>1</quantity>
                    <size>XL</size>
                    <color>green</color>
                    <unit_price>$59.99</unit_price>
                </item>
```

```
<item code="36671">
    <description>Calbert Climb Slim Fit Jeans
        </description>
    <quantity>1</quantity>
    <size>
        <waist>32</waist>
        <leg>28</leg>
    </size>
    <color>black</color>
    <unit_price>$49.99</unit_price>
</item>
        </shopping_cart>
    </content>
</page>
```

When the site is first created, a sample shopping cart can be created and saved as a static XML file, allowing the XSLT style sheet designer to design the "View Shopping Cart" page. In the meantime the programmers develop a shopping cart application with an object that outputs an XML representation of the cart using the XML tag structure. As a first step they create a JavaServer Page (JSP) or Active Server Page (ASP) that simply writes out the same dummy XML as in the static page and uses it to replace the static XML file. When the shopping cart functionality is done, they can modify the JSP or ASP page so that it gets the data from the shopping cart object and dynamically generates the XML. Immediately the dynamic XML is integrated with the Web site, with the same layout and formatting as for the dummy XML page. The XSLT style sheet doesn't know the difference between the static and dynamic XML.

The asynchronous development process is summarized in this table.

Development Style	Programmer	Style Sheet Designer
Paired	✧ Agree on XML structure for particular content section ✧ Create static dummy XML file ✧ Create simple XSLT templates to display dummy XML and add to master style sheet	

Development Style	Programmer	Style Sheet Designer
Asynchronous	✧ Draft schema document ✧ Add unit test to validate new XML against DTD ✧ Replace static dummy XML file with code module that statically outputs same dummy XML ✧ Interface with business objects, replace dummy XML with dynamic data	✧ Rework initial templates to reformat page layout ✧ Add graphical elements ✧ Develop DHTML interface enhancements

Dummy XML

The use of dummy XML as a placeholder for XML content is good practice. In fact, it is often useful to insert it in static content pages before the actual copy is available. We have developed a practice of starting off all of our pages with a few lines of Latin. Our dummy XML files are very simple, as shown here:

```
<page name="about_us">
      <title>About Us</title>
      <content>
        <p>Lorem ipsum dolor sit amet, consetetur sadipscing
elitr,  sed diam nonumy eirmod tempor invidunt ut labore et
dolore magna aliquyam erat, sed diam voluptua. At vero eos et
accusam et justo duo dolores et ea rebum.</p>

        <p>Stet clita kasd gubergren, no sea takimata sanctus
est Lorem ipsum dolor sit amet. Lorem ipsum dolor sit amet,
consetetur sadipscing elitr,  sed diam nonumy eirmod tempor
invidunt ut labore et dolore magna aliquyam erat, sed diam
voluptua.  At vero eos et accusam et justo duo dolores et ea
rebum.</p>

        <p>Stet clita kasd gubergren, no sea takimata sanctus
est Lorem ipsum dolor sit amet. Lorem ipsum dolor sit amet,
consetetur sadipscing elitr,  sed diam nonumy eirmod tempor
```

```
invidunt ut labore et dolore magna aliquyam erat, sed diam
voluptua. At vero eos et accusam et justo duo dolores et ea
rebum. Stet clita kasd gubergren, no sea takimata sanctus est
Lorem ipsum dolor sit amet.
        </p>
    </content>
</page>
```

Greeking

Inserting meaningless dummy text as a placeholder for content is called "Greeking" and is very common in page layout. The "Lorem ipsum" phrase we use appears often in this context and has been used in the publishing industry for this purpose for many years.

At first dummy text may seem unnecessary. Why not simply wait until the real copy is available? In fact, we consider "Greeking" an important part of our process. What we do is to start developing a site by creating a dummy XML file for every page in the initial site map. At the same time, we start off with a simple and generic XSLT style sheet that transforms the dummy pages into HTML using a very generic and bland design.

Menus

The style sheet also generates menus that allow you to click on links that take you from one page to the next. It contains a number of *navigation templates,* which use the XML site map to build these menus. We haven't mentioned the XML site map until now, but it is an important ingredient in an XML site architecture and will be discussed in more detail soon. The site map ties all of the separate content files together.

Continuous Integration

Initially creating a collection of dummy XML files and generic style sheets makes it easy to create a skeletal prototype of the Web site during the first iteration. This prototype contains placeholders for each of the pages initially identified in the first version of the site map and tells how to navigate between them. Basically it provides a starting point for all future development. Meaningful content, dynamic functionality, sophisticated navigation, and stylized design are added by changing the various style sheets and XML pages.

In this way the architecture supports a sort of continuous integration process. What we mean by this is that at all times a complete working site can be browsed in entirety without errors. At first the site will contain meaningless information and have a bland design, but as work is done on it, the style sheets and dynamic or static content pages are updated so that the site evolves from skeletal to fully fleshed.

Continuous integration keeps customers involved in and informed about the progress of a project, in keeping with XP practices. Once an initial site map has been drafted, the site skeleton can be created rapidly with minimal effort. It can then be deployed on the preview Web server by the end of the first iteration and presented to the customer. The skeleton may not look impressive, but it can still be considered an actual deliverable. Moreover, as development continues, it gradually evolves into a dynamic, attractive site whose progress can be shown to the customer at the end of each iteration. Finally, because of the aforementioned asynchronicity between design, content development, and programming, progress is continual and demonstrable.

Having an initial functionally navigable skeleton during the first iteration starts things off on the right foot, providing the structural framework for the rest of the project. As programmers and content developers continuously replace dummy XML code with new XML content and dynamic data, they immediately see this new material integrated into the site, with proper design and formatting in accordance with the current style sheet. This makes it natural for them to adhere to the first law of XML development and eliminates any temptation to revert to HTML encoding.

The XML Site Map

Let's take a few minutes to look closely at the structure of a sample site map.[1] We will see some examples of its use with navigation templates in an XSLT style sheet to combine XML pages into a cohesive site.

Navigation

Navigation is a key element in all sites design because Web sites are organized into sections and subsections, each of which consists of any number of pages. Every Web site uses menus and links to allow the user to find and display the content he is looking for. Content and navigation are the two most important pieces of information on a Web page. There are many books that will teach you how to use an XSLT style sheet to transform a page of XML content into formatted HTML, but this is not enough to turn a collection of XML pages into an entire Web site. The most important knowledge is how to use XML and XSL to create the navigation components necessary to link the pages in an organized and systematic way.

We have developed a simple and elegant navigation scheme that with a few basic XSLT tricks, allows entire Web sites to be driven dynamically by XSLT. The steps to achieve this are as follows:

✧ Assign each page in your Web site a unique name. This includes dynamic code-driven pages.

---

1. This section will be understood best by readers who have some familiarity with XSLT and XPATH. We explain how XSLT templates work, but readers who have had no exposure to XSLT will find it very useful to refer to a book on the topic.

- ✧ Create an XML site map.

- ✧ Create an XML file for each page. Each page should have a root element with a name attribute corresponding to its name in the site map. Dynamic pages should output XML with the same root <page> element—for example, <page name="about_us">...</page>.

- ✧ Create an XSLT style sheet with templates for formatting the various content types.

- ✧ Add navigation templates to the XSLT style sheet that read the site map and display menus and links appropriate for the current location in the Web site.

It is easy to create navigation templates in XSLT that are "context sensitive" in the sense that they can determine where the current page is in the site map and display local menus for the current subsection. A simple example of this is "Back" and "Next" buttons that you can create dynamically by having your XSLT template set up links to adjacent pages.

Site Map Structure

The XML site map is the backbone of your site. It defines the site structure and groups pages into a hierarchical set of menus, sections, and subsections. The site map uses a simple recursive nested structure, as shown here:

```
<?xml version='1.0'?>
<?xml-stylesheet type="text/xsl" ?>
<sitemap>
    <menu type="main">
        <page name="products">
            <title>Products</title>
            <content src="/product_browse.asp"/>
        </page>
        <page name="store_locator">
            <title>Store Locator</title>
            <content src="/store_locator/default.xml"/>
```

```xml
                        <page name="store_details" hidden="true">
                            <title>Store Details</title>
                            <content src="/store_locator/default.xml"/>
                        </page>
                    </page>
                    <page name="about_us">
                        <title>About Us</title>
                        <content src="/about_us/default.xml"/ >
                        <page name="our_history">
                            <title>Our History</title>
                            <content src="/about_us/our_history.xml"/>
                        </page>
                        <page name="in_the_community">
                            <title>In The Community</title>
                            <content src="/about_us/
                                in_the_community.xml"/>
                        </page>
                    </page>
                    <page name="our_partners">
                        <title>Our Partners</title>
                        <content src="/our_partners/default.xml"/>
                    </page>
                    <page name="flyers" hidden="true">
                        <title>Flyers</title>
                        <content src="/flyers/thanks.xml"/>
                    </page>
                </menu>
                <menu type="global">
                    <page name="privacy_policy">
                        <title>Privacy Policy</title>
                        <content src="/global/privacy_policy.xml"/>
                    </page>
                    <page name="contact_us">
                        <title>Contact Us</title>
                        <content src="/global/contact_us.xml"/>
                    </page>
                    <page name="career_opportunities">
                        <title>Career Opportunities</title>
                        <content src="/global/
                                    career_opportunities.xml"/>
                    </page>
                    <page name="feedback">
                        <title>Feedback</title>
                        <content src="/global/feedback.xml"/>
                    </page>
                </menu>
            </sitemap>
```

Notice that our site map consists of a number of menu definitions, denoted by <menu> elements each of which contains several pages. The first element has attribute type="main" and the second, smaller one has type="global". The main menu is a basic tree structure, with some pages nested under the home page and additional pages and subpages nested under these. There are also a few important pages that appear as links on every page of the site and don't fit into any one place in the main hierarchical tree. These are organized in a global group separate from the main group. Many sites contain one main menu and one or two flat global menus that appear at the top or bottom of every page. The main menus often have a hierarchical structure a few levels deep, while the global menus usually contain a small number of links to important pages such as copyright information, legal disclaimers, and contact information.

Each menu contains <page> elements. Pages in the main menu contain nested <page> elements, which represent site sections or subsections. This recursive structure supports site map trees of arbitrary depth, although most moderate-sized sites are only a few levels deep.

Using the Site Map

In order to use the XML site map you need to read it into the XSLT style sheet by declaring a couple of XSLT variables called sitemap and current_page.

```
<xsl:variable name="sitemap" select="document('../
sitemap.xml')/sitemap"/>
<xsl:variable name="current_page" select="$sitemap//
page[@name=current()/page/@name]"/>
```

The declaration reads the map by calling the XSLT document() function and sets its value as a reference to the map's root element, which is called sitemap. The current_page variable finds the page node within the site map whose name attribute is the same as that of the root "page element of the current page." Once these values have been initialized, it is easy to generate a simple menu like the one that follows.

XML creates order out of chaos.

```
<xsl:template name="main_menu ">
    <xsl:for-each select="$sitemap/menu[@type=main]/page >
        <a class="menu">
            <xsl:attribute name="href">
                <xsl:value-of select="content/@src"/>
            </xsl:attribute>
            <xsl:value-of select="title"/>
        </a>
        <xsl:if test="following-sibling::page"> | </xsl:if>
    </xsl:for-each>
</xsl:template>
```

The template loops through all of the top-level page elements that are children of the <menu type="main"> element. It prints out each page title with a link to the page in a horizontal row separated by a vertical bar. You can call this template from another template in the style sheet by writing

```
<xsl:template match="/page">
    <table name="main_menu">
        <tr>
            <td>Main Menu:</td>
        </tr>
        <tr>
            <td><xsl:call-template name="main_menu"></td>
        </tr>
```

```
    </table>
<xsl:apply-templates select="content"/>
```

Unit Testing with XML

XML and XSLT open up a wide variety of unit-testing possibilities.[2] With XML you can test that a file is *well formed* (i.e., that it conforms to the basic rules of XML structure) simply by checking if it can be read by an XML parser without generating an error. As discussed earlier, validating parsers and schema documents can be used for this purpose. Beyond structure validation, test scripts can be written that use an XML parser to examine the contents of a file and ensure that text nodes and attributes contain the appropriate values.

Unit testing can be done on an XML file both *before* and *after* its transformation by an XSLT style sheet. Before the XSLT is applied, you can test the raw XML data to ensure that it contains the correct information and is properly structured. After the XSLT is applied, you can test the output to ensure that the transformation succeeded and that the resulting output is properly formatted.

Output Methods

Testing XSLT output is easy if you set the output method of the style sheet to xml. XSLT supports three output methods: xml, html, and text, which you can set with the <xsl:output> element. Even though you are transforming your source XML into HTML, you can set the output to XML, which will basically result in an XHTML document that can be loaded into your XML parser.

Testing Options

Once you have loaded your output XHTML into your XML parser, there are a number of things you can do with it. As a first

---

2. See Chapter 14 for a full discussion of unit testing.

XML versus HTML: Image Tags

One example of the difference in setting your style sheet to XML rather than HTML is a template that contains an image tag. In XML you must have matching opening or closing tags. Thus, a pair of tags with no content (e.g., `<x></x>`) can be written with an empty tag notation that uses a slash following the tag name (e.g., `<x />`). An XML parser treats both of these notations as equivalent. An HTML image tag is written as `<img src="">`, which violates the XML matching tag rule. In the source code of your XSLT style sheet, you specify an image in the output as `<img src="" />`, but if the output method is set to HTML, the XSLT processor converts `<img src="" />` to an old-fashioned `<img src="">`. If you attempt to load this output document into an XML parser, it will generate an error, but if the output method is set as `xml`, the result will be a proper XHTML `<img src="" />` tag.

step you can test that it conforms to the XHTML specification by validating it against one of the XHTML DTDs. (You can download these DTDs from *http://www.w3.org/TR/xhtml1/*.)

You can also check for the existence and structure of various elements on the page by inserting element IDs into your XSLT templates so that the elements can be quickly retrieved and tested. For example, a template that inserts a banner ad at the top of a page can write it as

```
<img  id="banner ad" src=""ad7.gif" width="" height=""
onClick="bannerClick()"/>
```

To verify that the XSL properly inserted the ad, a unit test can be written that uses the parser API to find a node containing the attribute `id="banner ad"`. The test can check that the height and width attribute values are correct, or it can perform a link check on the image's `src` attribute to make sure that the image is there.

Another possibility for unit testing is enforcing policies for using Cascading Style Sheets (CSSs). CSSs can (and should) be used with the XHTML output of XSLT style sheets in much the same way they are used with standard HTML Web sites. CSSs and XSLT go well together, with XSLT used to lay out a page and CSSs applied to various page elements by adding `class` attributes. As long as the XHTML page generated by the XSLT contains a link to a CSS, that CSS will be applied by the browser. In any project using CSSs, sloppy HTML or XSLT designers are often tempted to slip in a little `bgcolor` attribute here and a `<font>` tag there rather than define a new CSS class. Now that we are loading our XHTML into an XML parser, we can write unit tests that look for these abominations in an XHTML page and generate errors any time they appear.

XSLTUnit

Up until now we have been discussing ways to perform unit tests on an entire XHTML Web page from a site. A unit test queries the Web server and retrieves a page, with all of its content, and performs test on it. Another approach to unit testing XSLT is for the test function itself to transform some XML code with a style sheet and perform tests on the results. In this way you can write tests that elicit exact results, right down to the text contents of the output. This is the approach taken by XSLTUnit, a generic XSLT unit testing tool, available for download from *http://xsltunit.org/*.

The currently posted version of XSLTUnit is 0.1. Described by its author as a "proof of concept" at this stage, it shows promise for being developed into a robust and powerful tool.

XSLTUnit supports the writing of unit tests themselves in XSLT. It contains a library of templates that are called by the test style sheet, and it provides two basic testing methods: matching the output against some expected reference XML and XPATH tests.

One advantage of XSLTUnit is that it can test individual templates within a larger style sheet by passing to that style sheet small XML snippets that correspond to a small part of a complete XML Web page. Once these snippets are passed to the XSLT, just the templates that are designed to transform them are invoked, thereby allowing a more targeted unit test.

Deploying the XML Site

There are a number of tools available to deploy XML- and XSLT-based Web sites on various platforms. We will discuss a few of them here.

The Microsoft XSL ISAPI filter is a plug-in for IIS that can be configured to perform on-the-fly XSLT processing of XML files and ASP pages. It uses MSXML—Microsoft's XML parser, which contains a fast XSLT processor—and caching and precompilation of the XSLT for excellent performance. Another feature is that it allows you to specify different style sheets for different browser types or version numbers. The XML ISAPI filter is downloadable for free from the XML section of the MSDN Web site at *http://msdn.microsoft.com*.

The Apache XML project has two subprojects for XML-based Web publishing, Cocoon and Ax-Kit. Cocoon is a Java-based framework for building and deploying XML and XSLT sites. It is available at *http://xml.apache.org/cocoon*. Ax-Kit is implemented in Perl and available at *http://axkit.org*. A simple Java servlet filter similar in principle to the Microsoft XML ISAPI and available for use with JSP and Apache can be downloaded from *http://www.servletsuite.com/servlets/xmlflt.htm*.

Part IV

Web XP Best Practices

XP clearly addresses the fundamental issues facing Web teams—risk, change, and trust—which translate perfectly from software to the Web. The question is how it deals with Web development's day-to-day practices. This part presents many of XP's practices and invents some new ones to show how Web projects can make XP their own.

Chapter 11

Planning

It is a bad plan that admits of no modification
—Publilius Syrus

XP planning is not about knowing the future but about not knowing it. Iterative development and continuous integration minimize the impact of constant change and bank the winnings of each iteration.

Software development has been described as similar to driving in that both involve continuous small heading adjustments. We like to think of it as a game of golf in that you have a goal but you may not see it. Your customer can tell you that the goal is 400 feet and just around the dogleg ahead. Your experienced team members may have been on a hole like this before and can warn you of risks like sand traps and water hazards along the way. How hard will you hit the ball? Will you hit it just right? Will the wind carry it away from where you are aiming? Is the customer wrong about where the hole is? Is there a hazard that your team doesn't know about?

Our golf analogy can stretch a long way. Immediately we see that, like golf, Web projects have a number of associated risks:

- ✧ The project manager and his ability to get good estimates from the team

- ✧ The customer and what she wants from the project

- ✧ The business changes and other unseen obstacles that can affect the project

High Risk versus High Cost

Before XP there were two approaches. Going with the golf analogy, the first was to hit that ball as hard as you could until you got to the hole or until the customer determined that you had no hope of ever reaching it. The second was to document every possible attribute of the course, every possible risk, and every possible contingency for every stroke on the way to the hole. The first involved high risk; the second, high cost. Which would you choose?

When you don't know the scope of a project,
selecting a price is a high-risk undertaking.

The XP Alternative

XP is a third way. To use it you need to accept the following three premises:

- ✦ Estimates are guesses. There are too many variables and unknowns in a complex project to make more than sweeping estimates of how long things will take and at what cost.

- ✦ The customer can't describe what is required in the detail your team needs up front. The project itself will greatly influence the customer's requirements and customers will change their minds as the project proceeds.

- ✦ There are business factors beyond the project manager's or customer's foresight. Team members will leave, the market in which the project was to be launched will change, and priorities will fluctuate.

XP planning is important, but keep in mind that the long-term plan, the release plan, is a guideline, not a contract.[1] Our experience in using XP for Web project planning has shown that you need to take account of six essential elements:

- ✦ Iterations
- ✦ User stories
- ✦ Project velocity
- ✦ The Team
- ✦ Communications
- ✦ Adapting XP for the Web

---

1. See Chapter 4 for a full discussion of release planning.

Iterations

Our general advice is to keep iterations small. Think of building a Web site as rock climbing, with the length of an iteration similar to the distance between each safety stop you hammer into the rock face. There is overhead attached to stopping and hammering in a piton, just as there is in each iteration strategy and planning session, and this overhead tempts people to extend the period between each safety stop and press on. The best way to determine the optimum stopping point is to decide how far you are willing to fall. There is a distance that is so short that not enough has changed to bother replanning. There is also a distance that is so long that a fall can be fatal.

In XP we want to find a sweet spot. From the customer to your own team, short iterations keep you out of trouble by finding problems early and giving everyone an opportunity to continuously reevaluate priorities and requirements.

Iterations are safety stops, where teams can reestimate; they
also give teams a sense of accomplishment.

Keep to Two-Week Iterations and Independent Stories

We recommend that Web projects follow a two-week iteration schedule. This is good because it allows you to work on a number of stories across the Web site without having to include one that depends on another. When one story depends on another story, your team cannot start working on the dependent story until the first one is finished. At the very least you will find that the unforeseen risks of the first story are present in related stories. When we first started using XP, we planned a number of stories in an iteration that depended on each other. By doing so we reintroduced the risk of our old waterfall process. When the first story in the chain took twice the time we estimated, the resulting delays cascaded into every other story, and at the end of the iteration we had very little to show for our time. However, when we planned iterations with stories that were completely unrelated, we could run into serious trouble on one story and still deliver all the others.

Why not one week? There is no reason that you cannot do one-week iterations, but we steer away from them because they provide too little room to move. Stories that turn out to be longer than estimated still get done in a two-week iteration, whereas in a one-week iteration they have to be dropped. The graphic design process calls for a number of stories that consistently take two weeks. Moreover, few customers have the time to do iteration meetings every week. Finally there are the intangibles, including the bigger sense of accomplishment to be had from the deliverables of a two-week iteration than from a single week. Your experience may vary but we have found that two weeks is a long enough iteration to make good progress without adding unnecessary risk.

Plan Iteration Strategy

For us every iteration starts with two key meetings: first the iteration strategy meeting followed immediately by the iteration planning meeting. To simplify this process with customers, we book these meetings at the beginning of the project, for the entire project. Because we know that every iteration will be exactly two weeks long, we know exactly when these meetings will be held. This reduces the amount of scheduling problems in the future.

The Strategy Meeting

The focus of the strategy meeting is on the overall goal and direction of the project. Customer, strategist, project manager, design lead, and technical lead attend—all of the key people who will help the customer develop stories and provide a goal for the coming iteration.

The first task of this meeting is to write new stories or change existing ones. This is done not only by the customer but also by team members. At the beginning of the project, more stories will be developed by the team than by the customer, but as the project goes on the customer will write more and more. For each story the team will provide a ballpark estimate, whose purpose is to provide the customer with a rough idea of the amount of work involved.

The next step is defining the metrics for success. Try asking the following questions:

- ✧ Will this story generate traffic?
- ✧ Will this story generate new revenue or increase existing revenue?
- ✧ Will this story help change patterns of behavior?
- ✧ Will this story help reduce costs?

By discussing the amount of work a feature involves and its benefits or drawbacks, the customer can assign a priority to each story.

The Planning Meeting

The goal of the *planning meeting* is to involve the team in the process and more clearly define what will be done in the coming iteration. Everyone involved in the project attends. The meeting begins with the review of stories that the customer wishes to complete. Every person on the team can ask whatever questions they need answered to gain a full understanding of what the customer is requesting.

For each story the team assesses all of the tasks necessary to complete the story along with the potential risks and maps out possible solutions to these risks. As content delivery is the most frequent cause of delay in Web site development, we define the content requirements at this point to help the customer understand the ramifications of delivering late.

When the development team fully understands what is expected from each story, they provide their estimates for how long stories will take to complete. Allowing the team to volunteer for stories is critical.

At the end of the iteration, with all of the information reviewed and the estimates tallied, it is time for the customer to make decisions, this time, on what they want to do in the following iteration.

To get approval on the final plan, the project manager produces a simple document listing the stories the customer has chosen for the team to work on along with the estimated time each will take to complete and the total number of hours the iteration will require.

Plan for Width Before Depth

Web sites can be wide and deep. Wide refers to the number of unrelated functions to be found on a site, and deep refers to the complexity of those functions. When possible take advantage of the width to vary the stories in an iteration. This is better for the customer because when the team focuses on one function and runs deep on it in one or two iterations, the customer loses the opportunity to evolve the application. The customer will give better input to the team if an application comprising five stories is delivered one story per iteration over five iterations rather than five in one. In general we recommend that, say, five pieces of functionality in a Web project be built a story at a time over a number of iterations. Doing this allows the team to explore risks early in the process by doing the riskiest stories for all functions; it also lets the customer re-evaluate requirements as he sees the project unfold.

Make Customer Input Easy and Controllable

Short iterations are also a good customer management strategy. Imagine walking into your first iteration planning meeting and asking a new customer to decide on a month's worth of work. You will invoke paralysis. Further, you are asking for more trust than may exist so early on. Many of your customers will not be used to the iterative process and will be feeling uneasy about starting the project without the reams of design documents they are accustomed to. Take it slow and prove the merits of XP in short easy-to-digest chunks with ample time for deliberation and feedback.

Ask any Web developer what railroads every project and she will tell you it is waiting for content from the customer. On most projects the customer is responsible for delivering either the copy or approval of it. He also needs to get you database schemas of legacy applications, corporate logos, contact information, and other Web site content. Before XP we would generate a list of everything we needed and wait for the customer to deliver. And wait, and wait.

Using XML you can press on with a project without much content, but you still can't launch without it. That's why short iterations are good—they let the customer deliver small parts of the content every two weeks. With small homework assignments, the odds of keeping a continuous pace are much higher. You also reduce risk by determining quickly if the customer is going to be able to do his part. Once he misses a small delivery, you quickly learn that you have a problem and can work out a new strategy to get the content.

In many cases you are getting content from more than one customer on a project. When you find out who delivers and who doesn't, you can reorganize delivery to shift more critical responsibility to proven performers. If the customer is hopeless, you can send a team member to his office to gather the content or hire a writer to do the bulk of the job.

Keep Track of Tasks

Once the customer has approved the iteration plan, the team starts work on the stories. Each story is posted at the top of the project board with associated tasks listed below. Every morning the team meets to walk through each task. At the first stand-up meeting of the iteration, team members volunteer for tasks by estimating how long they think they will take to complete. Every day they report on their progress, updating their estimates and discussing any problems. As tasks are completed they are crossed off the list. This boosts team morale and makes both the project manager and the customer happy.

Keep the Customer Involved in Delivery

After two weeks an iteration is over, which means that it is time to meet to present the deliverables. Since a story isn't completed until it has been proven, this includes walking the customer through any stories that she has not approved; the meeting cannot end without customer approval. Any story not approved by the customer is considered incomplete and is postponed to a later iteration. As early as possible before the end of the iteration, the project manager should advise the customer if a story will not be completed by that time.

User Stories

At the beginning of each iteration, the development team and the customer will meet to define the work to be completed in it, through the development of "user stories." A user story is a user experience or action on a Web site written on an index card—for example, executing a keyword search. Each description is usually one to three sentences.

Keep iteration stories in a highly visible area where there
is room for daily standup meetings.

In XP the customer develops the user stories; however, in Web
XP stories are frequently created by programmers, designers, strategists, and project managers. This happens largely because the customer is unaware that a feature can be implemented or that a story
is needed by the Web development process. Here are some examples
of stories generated by the development team:

⬥ Create a color palette for the Web site that includes color
  combinations, rules for use, and RGB and hex code values.

⬥ Create a tool that allows the customer to run multiple sur-
  veys concurrently.

There are many recommendations for writing good stories. The
ones we have found to be the most useful include those discussed in
the following sections.

Stories Should Be Written in a Language That the Customer Understands

Don't write stories that read like an advanced developer's guide to information architecture. Keep them simple, in plain words. If possible, if you have seen the feature on another Web site, reference its location.

Stories Should Provide the Customer with Something Tangible

Don't write stories that won't create anything once completed. At the end of the iteration, you will need to present a deliverable for every story that you agreed could be completed.

Stories Should Take between One and Two Weeks to Complete

Ideally you should be able to complete several stories in an iteration, so make sure that the length of each story suits that time frame. Kent Beck recommends that stories take between one and five programming weeks.[2] We have shortened this to a maximum of two weeks, but it really is up to you. If a story is estimated to take longer, this is a sign that you should break it into smaller stories. If it is shorter than one week, try to combine it with another small story.

Stories Must Be Testable

At the end of every iteration, you must prove not only that the story has been completed but that it works. This is much easier for programming stories than for creative stories. Sometimes automated tests can be created and run by the customer at the end of an iteration. Sometimes the deliverable is more subjective, such as a mood board. In these cases the customer should agree up front that the deliverable alone is proof that the story has been completed.

---

2. See Beck, K. *Extreme Programming Explained*. Boston: Addison-Wesley, 2000, p. 179.

Once you have written a story, you will need to assess its priority, risk, type, and whether it involves creative, interface, or server-side development and dependencies. It is not recommended that stories be dependent on each other, but this is sometimes impossible to avoid in Web development.

With all of the information collected, the next step is figuring out what can be done in one iteration. This will be a team effort, with input from both the developers and the customer. If you end up with stories that have dependencies, make sure that they are not scheduled in the same iteration.

Once you have finalized which stories are scheduled for this iteration, save the rest for future iterations. We use a "story box" for each customer, in which we store all of the user stories created for a given project. The box is organized by iteration and allows us to easily flip through and see when stories were completed and what is left to schedule.

There are many benefits of developing user stories, but our favorite is that they eliminate the need for thick requirements documents. Web customers rarely have the time or the patience to read through those documents anyway. Also, requirements change, and no one wants to go back and rewrite them. Stories are so much better because they are easy to create and can be reevaluated at each iteration.

Project Velocity

Project velocity is a tangible metric of the pace at which the team can produce deliverables. It is based on actual performance, not wishful thinking. When velocity slips, the team needs to find out why and fix it. Everyone on the team is accountable. If a team is able to do five stories this iteration and only two the next, there is a problem that needs to be solved. Were there less ideal work hours this iteration? If so, why? Did everyone put in a full work week?

Continuous integration may seem slower, but you will
soon see that it makes projects go faster.

The project you are working on may have a business requirement
to achieve a certain velocity, in which case the project manager
needs to define a team size to accommodate this pace so that members work a reasonable and consistent amount from iteration to iteration. Keep your stories somewhat equal in work effort. Wild
variations in story size make tracking velocity very difficult.

Whether you have a required velocity or a fixed team size, your
goal is to develop consistency and predictability. Your customer
needs to know how much she can count on receiving from your
team in each iteration and at what cost.

Estimating Velocity

Velocity is not a set function of the number of team members
times work hours equaling some number of lines of code or pages.
It can be assessed only after a number of iterations as a function

of the individual scope that can be completed by each member of the team.

We use "yesterday's weather" to make our predictions about how the team will perform in the future. That is, we start with a guess, see what happens, and use the results as our next guess. If stories are approximately equal in scope and complexity, then the number of "ideal development hours" (hours of noninterrupted work) that it takes to do the first ten stories should be the same for the next ten stories.

It takes a number of iterations to figure this out because tracking an actual ideal development hour can be tricky. Most of the things that cut into ideal time should be removed in the first few iterations. Then estimates become more predictable when each developer can see her own patterns. Many meteorologists today use history in their predictions. They look at the last 100 days on which conditions were the same as on the current day. If it rained on 30 of those 100 days, then the chance of rain is 30 percent.

Why Is Velocity Important?

Nervous customers make life hell for the team. A consistent velocity that predictably delivers functionality every two weeks puts the customer at ease. If the velocity is not adequate, the customer has the option of increasing the budget and adding team members. If you are going to negotiate with a customer over how much he can expect from a team, you have to be able to show a consistent project velocity and back it up with estimates and actuals. You should be able to do this by tracking the first three iterations.

Changing Velocity

What happens when three people leave the team and are replaced by new staff? What happens when the programming language is changed? How will this effect velocity? Such changes will definitely have an effect but how much is unknowable. Changes to the team or to the nature of the project will impact the project in unpredictable ways. Only after measuring a number of iterations will you have a clear picture of this impact and be able to establish a new project velocity.

The Team

XP works well when team members can let go of ownership of their own work and take on ownership for the whole project. XP encourages this, but some manipulation by a clever project manager never hurts.

We recommend a number of pairings among disciplines on the team. To pass information and new skills quickly to everyone on the project we want as many parings as possible.

As project manager you are going to let your team members volunteer for stories. Once you have assigned a few stories to each member you get everyone to volunteer to be helpers on stories. Make suggestions on who can help out on which stories based on a number of factors, which are described next.

Relevant Experience

Suggest a helper who has done a similar story or has experience in the particular language. These people will generally identify themselves.

Diversity

Everyone brings a new pair of eyes to an application. Try to get as many members of the team working on a function as possible. This takes some forethought, and these pairing generally do not occur naturally. Still, the more people who touch a piece of work, the more you add to the quality of the end product.

Skills Transfer

Junior people should work with senior people, and designers should work with programmers. You may meet with some resistance here. Senior programmers usually don't want to work with less experienced staff—only a few want to be mentors. This disinclination may disappear over time as senior staff see their own skills improve in the process of teaching newcomers. To begin with, however, many of these pairings will have to be dictated by the project manager.

The People Skills of the Project Manager

Project managers need to be good judges of character. Some team members will click with each other and you will get a lot out of these pairings. Others may erupt into World War III. Try out new couplings, but find a balance between mixing it up and tuning your team for peak efficiency.

Communications

Keeping the team informed about the progress of the project is essential to success and adds to the members' sense of project ownership. The problem is that everyone wants to get on with his own tasks, and meetings, which are often seen as time wasters, are not popular. The solution we have developed is the use of regular, short, standup meetings.

We do a 15-minute standup meeting every morning. A corkboard has all the story cards for an iteration on it. We use it to discuss the stories the team worked on the previous day and to get a brief status report on how they are coming along. We revise the time estimate for current stories and reevaluate if the new estimates will require us to drop some stories from the iteration or allow us to add more. In either case the customer selects which stories to add or remove.

All members of the team are at the daily standup meeting and report on how they are doing. We find that discussion of the stories creates tangential discussions. Important ones tend to move into a room with a white board immediately after the standup meeting, while the trivial ones fizz out once the meeting breaks up.

Adapting XP

No process, including XP, is the silver bullet for every team or every project. XP is a good idea that many development teams have used and had successes with. However, sometimes in our exuberance with our own results we make statements that sound like holy writ. This is not our intention.

This book itself is a departure from normal XP practices and a good example of where XP needs adjustments to make it relevant to Web development. We have made a blanket statement that Web projects are different from software projects and that there is a need to adapt XP practices to suit the needs of a multidisciplinary team.

We encourage everyone using XP for software projects, Web projects, or home gardening projects to try to understand the process, give its practices a chance, and then pick what works. Sometimes this is a gradual process.

When we started using XP we couldn't get past the lack of documentation. We still required the team to produce UML documents such as activity and class diagrams. Only after seeing unit tests in action and the stories generated from a CRC session were we able to let go.[3]

In other areas we still have problems accepting XP as dogma. For example, XP places the responsibility for writing stories squarely on the customer. However, in Web projects customers are not the domain experts we need, so stories are written primarily by a strategist or project manager. Customers still set priorities and aid in strategy development, but this is not the traditional XP story writing practice.

---

3. See Chapter 12 for a full discussion of CRC.

In spite of our reservations, Kent Beck has not excommunicated us from XP and Martin Fowler doesn't call us at three in the morning making threats. That said, we feel comfortable telling you to use XP when it works and not to use it when it doesn't. The real promise of a good process is that it can give birth to an even better one.

Chapter 12

Design

Our life is frittered away by detail . . . Simplify, simplify.
—Henry David Thoreau

Design is not a phase of a project that gives way to a building phase. Design and creation are one and the same. XP stresses this interconnectedness and reduces the number of design documents to those that actually help developers develop.

The ultimate goal of development is a successful Web site that will enhance a customer's corporate image, attract users, and allow easy and satisfying navigation. We have found that Web site design requires some closely followed best practices to further this goal:

◇ Aim for simple, elegant code.

◇ Use CRC cards for design sessions.

◇ Use naming conventions to save time.

◇ Reduce risk by using prototypes.

- ✧ Start slowly.
- ✧ Don't plan for tomorrow.
- ✧ Refactor, refactor, refactor.

Simplicity

Over the years we have worked with many programmers with many different programming styles—the "fearful," who are afraid to ask questions and came up with crazy solutions; the "geniuses," who prove their ingenuity in their work; and that rare breed, the "simplicity seekers."

While everyone thinks we should feel privileged to be managing the geniuses, the ones we find the best by far are the simplicity seekers because they develop code that is simple and easy to figure out and thus elegant. They are geniuses in their own right for being able to keep a project from turning into an impossible mass of code.

CRC Cards

We started using Class Responsibilities and Collaboration (CRC) cards to design the objects we were developing. In our CRC sessions we defined each class on a big card and we mixed up the cards to show class responsibilities and collaborations. With movable cards we could easily see that multiple classes shared the same data access functions and so we would remove a method from 10 classes and make a new one to do the job for all.[1] At the end of these sessions we would stick the cards on the wall where the programmers work.

---

1. We highly recommend *Using CRC Cards: An Informal Approach to Object-Oriented Development* by Nancy M. Wilkinson, SIGS Books and Multimedia, 1995.

Soon we where using cards to represent a Web site. Cards could represent content on a page from an XML file, navigation on a page from an XSLT file, and the layout of the page from a cascading style sheet. From these exercises came the design patterns discussed in Chapter 8. Server-side programmers used cards to show interface programmers the interactions of servlets and DLLs with JSP and ASP pages. Database schemas were quickly developed using cards as well. It wasn't long before cards replaced all of our design tools.

CRC cards are great because they are disposable, are easy to move around, and can be transformed from conceptual to implementation tools by the simple addition of more information. For a team cards are great because they are big and can be stuck on the wall for all to see.

Naming Conventions

A few years ago one of us was working on a project where a programmer spent three hours looking for a graphic file. The programmer was working on a registration form and needed a "Submit" button. He asked a designer for the graphic, but neither thought to agree on what the image would be called or where it would be saved, so the designer put it in the same folder she was used to saving images in. The programmer waited an hour and then started to look for the file. After another hour he asked the designer if she had finished the graphic, which she had, but he still didn't ask where the file was and what it was called. The programmer then spent another hour searching through the entire project directory.

After speaking to the designer, we discovered that she was saving these images in a separate directory that the programmer knew nothing about, because she didn't know where else to save them.

This kind of problem can and should be avoided. At the beginning of each project, the team should discuss and agree to a directory structure and file naming conventions. It is even better if you can develop this kind of structure for all projects, making it easy for team members to switch from task to task *and* from project to project.

Remember to check frequently that the project directories are kept clean and that files are being named correctly.

Prototypes

Every Web project is just different enough from the one before. There is always a feature that you haven't done, some new navigation you would like to try, or something about the site's design that you aren't sure will work in all required browsers. How do you reduce the risk of these unknowns?

What works for us is prototypes. These can be anything from one HTML page to test a part of a design to a small program to test a piece of functionality. Whatever method you are using to verify that something will work, don't be quick to schedule the development in the same iteration. Try to keep the task you are testing to a future iteration just in case it can't be done.

Remember that prototypes are disposable. They are about learning something and have no other use. Never use prototype code in production code. Many people write their prototypes in a different programming language from the one used for production to help resist the temptation of reuse.

Starting Slowly

Keeping a project running smoothly depends on many factors, including how well the team works together. To identify problems early in the project, try to complete a few simple tasks before you attempt anything complicated. Any problem will be much clearer and easier to resolve at this point.

It is very important to sort out the people problems up front. It's better to deliver little in the first iteration and instead spend time solving issues with the team. That may seem wasteful at first, but it will pay you back. Think of it as insurance. Once you are working at full steam on complicated issues, you will have a hard time differentiating between an issue with the team and an issue with the code. But in the first few iterations, when your tasks are straightforward and low risk, team issues are easy to determine and less risky to solve than they will be six iterations later.

Changes

In Web site development tomorrow is never what you think it will be. Technologies will change, customers will change, and the next thing you know you will be building something very different from what you had been planning.

Try to keep your eyes on today and focus on what needs to be done in the current iteration only. Don't do anything that hasn't been asked of you and you will save yourself a lot of wasted time and energy.

Refactoring

Are you sure that what you programmed yesterday, last week, or last month was written the best possible way? Has this code since become redundant? If you agree that the best system is clean and uncluttered, then regular housecleaning will be required. Refactoring is the process of cleaning up the Web site. It is not just a programming task—everyone on the team will need to participate.

This essential step can be easily worked into your daily routines: As soon as you finish a task, step back and review what you did. Ask yourself: "Was there a better, more efficient way to do this?"

Over time Web site components become obsolete and the design needs to be updated. You will need to look back not just to earlier today but to yesterday, last week, and last month. At the end of each iteration, look at the Web site and ask yourself the following questions:

- Are there multiple objects doing the same thing?
- Is there code for functionality that has since been removed?
- Have the directory structure and naming conventions been followed?
- Is the site still easy to navigate?
- Is there enough room for the site's content?
- Does this site communicate the original vision?

Once you have the answers, you may have a list of tasks to complete. These should be written up as stories and suggested at the beginning of the next iteration.

Getting customers to agree to refactoring stories is an important milestone in your relationship with them. The first time you tell a customer that you want to spend her hours making the code better, be ready for trust alarms to go off. "Why didn't you write good code in the first place?" "All the tests passed; you're just gold plating."

Your first response might be to get very defensive. Don't. Explain that you wrote the code to make the test pass but now you want to make it better. Tell the customer what better means. If you can't, then you shouldn't be refactoring in the first place. In the end the customer makes the call.

Chapter 13

Coding

Coding is not typing! Coding is problem solving.

We find that there is a misconception about what it means to program. Coding is so much more than just sitting in front of the computer and typing. Coding is problem solving and requires a great deal of attention and creativity. There are so many obstacles to turning the design into code—from people walking by to asking questions to trying to find errors without any help.

Coding Best Practices

Over the last few years, Extreme Programming has developed some excellent best practices for the coding of software that apply very well to Web site development. These include the following:

⬥ Learn to love an onsite customer.

⬥ Write code to agreed standards.

Balancing the creation of unit tests and code
keeps the project from falling.

- ✧ Code the unit test first.
- ✧ Use paired development.
- ✧ Stick to continuous integration.
- ✧ Leave optimization until last.
- ✧ Avoid overtime.

Each of these practices will increase your productivity and the quality of what you produce.

Learn to Love an Onsite Customer

Much of what has been written about XP is targeted to internal IT departments, with the goal having a member of another department on the team. Imagine that person coming from another company altogether, with the added worry that how you are seen by her could affect the future of your company.

Certainly nothing in XP Web projects has been more resisted than working with an onsite customer. Having the person you have tried to impress so much in the sales process see how you actually operate can be alarming.

True, it is very frightening at first. But once the customer is in the group you will find that he is not a spy and that he has the same goal that you have. Any secrets he uncovers, like the fact that your company is a little smaller than you led him to believe or that your experience with a language is less than expert, are going to be less of a problem than you believe. We have found that customers are only going to care about one thing—can you do the job. If you can't, they are going to find that out, and if you can, they won't sweat the small stuff.

An onsite customer learns the processes, whereas one at arm's length never does. Also, understanding how you work, and what this work is, will make her a more realistic planner and far more accepting of the costs involved.

The final argument for an onsite customer is the efficiency she brings. Having someone there to approve a design, explain a business process, or suggest a way around problems drives the project faster.

Write Code to Agreed Standards

Far too many hours are wasted in trying to figure out what a programmer has done because code isn't in tabular format, or even trying to find where the graphic designer has saved headers or buttons. For this reason it is wise to develop a set of standards for coding, naming conventions, and directory structures. Make sure that you have a consensus on these standards before you start and then stick to them.

Code the Unit Test First

Writing unit tests is beneficial for many reasons, one being the great help they provide with the actual writing of code. Unit tests are an excellent tool for breaking down each programming task into "To Dos." Once you have finished your "To Dos," you will have finished your task.

Use Paired Development

Paired programming builds trust within the project team as well as between your company and your customer. Moreover, it increases overall skills development and speeds the work along.

Leave Optimization Until Last

According to XP you should always wait until you have finished a story and run your tests before you try to optimize your work. Only then can you analyze what exactly it is that needs optimizing. Don't make work for yourself by trying to anticipate problems before they exist—wait until you have the results of your analysis before you focus on resolving whatever issues arise.

Avoid Overtime

Avoiding overtime is as relevant to Web projects as it is to software. Everyone knows that you can never do your best work when

If you're sleeping at your desk, something has gone wrong!

you are tired or burnt out, because you are much more likely to make mistakes and you become less efficient, taking longer and longer to complete tasks.

If you find that you are putting in a lot of overtime, something has gone wrong in the planning of the project. If you have taken on too many stories, don't try to make up by working more hours. Instead, defer a story to the next iteration. Don't forget that the customer has agreed to an estimated number of hours, so overtime will affect her budget.

Chapter 14

Testing

Testing shouldn't wait until the project is finished. Start testing before you write one line of code. Test constantly and effectively and you will develop a much more durable Web site.

The term "debugging" comes from Harvard University in the 1950s. After an exhaustive search for an error in a program, engineers there opened up the computer and found that an insect had died in the innards, which was preventing a relay from closing. Once the bug was removed, the program worked perfectly. Since that time, *debugging* has meant the process of looking for and finding system errors.

Over the years, a mystical belief has evolved that bugs appear magically, by themselves. That belief is wrong. Errors occur because someone puts them there—all programmers create bugs.

How do the XP testing practices work in Web projects? To answer that question we need to look at

- ✧ Unit testing

- ✧ Unit tests for Web projects

- ✧ Unit tests for XML (see Chapter 9)

Unit Testing

In the past, bug hunting was done by testers and once the bug was discovered the programmer would remove the offending syntax. Now XP puts the primary responsibility back on the programmer for finding the bug that she created, through automated testing and build management. Quality assurance still has a major role in the testing process, but it is more "assurance" than babysitting.

Automated testing is done with unit tests. These are small programs that allow programmers to test methods in their object code on a pass/fail basis. Unit tests exist for almost every language. Here is how they work.

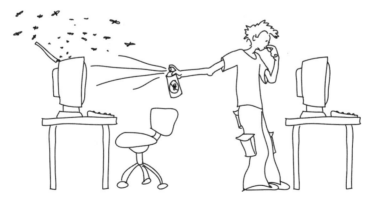

XP makes the programmer responsible for finding
and eliminating any bugs he created.

Before writing a single line of code, a programmer working on a story first writes a test for the function being created, in the same language she is using to write the program. The test needs to describe what the function will do. If the code doesn't perform its method correctly, it fails; if it does perform correctly, it passes. Very simple, but in this simplicity lies the cornerstone of all XP practices.

As systems get larger, they become brittle because a single change in one place can wreak havoc in others. The connections between objects become difficult to retrace as systems grow, and eventually touching any part of the code strikes fear into programmer's hearts. Refactor this code? Just try not to add four bugs for each one you remove and you are ahead of the average. If you are a manager, just try to get a programmer to take responsibility for code that someone else wrote.

Imagine the same system but with a unit test for each public method. Now when you make a change, you can see immediately where something has broken. You can tear out code and new methods without fear. The simple practice of unit testing extends the life of a system, uncouples the code from its author, and allows you to make code better over time instead of leaving it to decay.

XP is light on documentation. It can get away with this primarily because unit tests are the best documents you could ask for. Their parameters define perfectly the nature of the code, and the descriptions of how code can fail inherently describe how to make it pass in the simplest way.

Unit Tests for Web Projects

Unit testing for Web projects is almost identical to that for software development because most programs run on the server side. The difference is that, in the customer server environment used in Web projects, many programs will require input from and output to a remote customer, whether a browser, a PDA, or a device not yet available. The communication between the server object and the customer will be via HTTP over TCP/IP, which is why we need unit tests for browsers.

Unit tests can be written without HTTPUnit, but you will have to assume that the input from the customer is as you expected it to be. This is often necessary for programmers who are not working in Java.

Multiple Browsers

The most important nonfunctional requirement of any Web project is the browser you will support. Your unit tests are browser-independent, but the visual display of your site changes wildly from browser to browser and OS to OS. Even incrementally different versions of the same browser can behave in unpredictably different ways. In traditional software development, you code for one platform and when you are done you "port" the code to other platforms. In Web development you code for all platforms at the same time and all releases are to all platforms. This is the central problem of interface programming for the Web.

As we said before, Web projects can have teams of server-side programmers, interface programmers, project managers, graphic designers, copywriters, and customers.

Interface programming for the Web is a painful process. Assuming that programmers are using unit tests, testing how pages look and behave is the central job of your quality assurance people.

Server-Side Functionality Preferred

As a general rule you should keep as much functionality on the server as possible. Some years ago one of us created a shopping basket for a customer that required users to select the store at which they would pick up their purchases. We used JavaScript validation on the client side to ensure that they did this. Soon after launch customer service panicked because a number of orders had no store information. We figured out that many customers were using an old AOL browser that didn't support client-side JavaScript. Had we done server-side validation, this would not have happened.

The only part of the process that you have any real control over is the server, so you should take advantage of this when you can. Client-side validation makes sense for usability reasons, but your server code should not just assume that the customer's system is doing its job.

QA works from a "graphical style guide" and "storyboards" to determine if the Web site is displaying correctly and if the approved design has been used properly throughout the site. A number of tools on the market allow a single computer to view multiple browsers and versions. We use Vmware, which permits our QA workstations to connect to a Vmware server to toggle between multiple OSs and browsers. We do this because it is often not possible to run two versions of the same browser on one machine. Another, inexpensive way to do the same thing is to evenly distribute the range of browsers among your team and and have team members use a tool like VNC or PC Anywhere to test on each other's computers.

Choosing Browsers

What browsers should you support? The list of possibilities is endless, so we tell our customers to follow the 10 percent rule. Check the server logs from your existing site or use industry measurements, and support all browsers that are used by more than 10 percent of your users. Existing logs can tell you if your audience is different from the norm. For example, one of our customers publishes to the IT industry so usage of UNIX and Opera is significantly higher than overall browser usage averages.

Managing Assets

Managing the assets of a project over time can cause problems if not attended to early. All assets, including code, unit tests, graphics, diagrams, and the like, should be stored in one location, which should be governed by revision control software (RCS) such as CVS or Visual SourceSafe. In traditional software development, users check files into their own sandbox on the customer's computer or a directory on the server. In Web projects the development area needs to have a virtual directory for every team member.

Using CVS versus Visual SourceSafe

Most of our experience has been with CVS. It is a great tool because it is free, it has customers for multiple OSs, and it allows builds to be easily scripted with tools like Ant. Nevertheless, we are most comfortable working in Visual SourceSafe because of its close integration with Microsoft IDEs. Either product will do the job, but we recommend CVS for Java projects and Visual SourceSafe for Microsoft projects.

Users check files into their own sandbox
in traditional software development

All projects should conform to the same coding standards and file and directory naming conventions. Everyone should know what to call things and where to find them.

Web projects rely on an HTTP server and often an application server. Programmers need to see the results of their work instantly, and they can't be expected to check their code and do a build every time they want to see the results of a code change in a browser. Moreover, we cannot expect team members to run a Web server and application server on the customer's machine. Have you seen the licensing fees for some of these application servers?

The virtual directory that belongs to the user on the server needs to contain the complete Web site from the last working build and the files the user has checked out. Work in progress from another user should be kept in another virtual directory. All users should be able to make a change, save it without checking in, and reload their Web page to see the result.

RCS manages the checkin and checkout of files and can create a complete set of files from any point in time. A fully functioning copy—that is one that has passed all unit tests, Linkbot, and other automated tests of all the project files—is sent to a quality assurance (QA) folder for review.

QA reviews the site and uses a defect-tracking tool like Bugzilla to track errors and report them to the development team. Defect-tracking systems allow testers to report their finding to the team and track revisions from one "cut" (version of the project) to the next. Remember that the customer should be very much involved in this process. Bugs such as system crashes and bad data should be caught and fixed before the code ever gets near QA. If not, and these kinds of bugs are creeping up, you have to go back and write more unit tests. For defects that make it through QA, the customer should decide if they will be fixed or left alone for the time being. Every hour spent to fix a bug is an hour that could be spent on adding more functionality. The customer is the sole arbitrator of what is good enough!

It is true to say that automated testing on Web projects is still in its infancy. We can effectively test that all links work and that functions run correctly. XSL goes a long way to ensuring visual consistency throughout the site, but we are still overly reliant on human beings to say that everything is visually correct.

How to Get Started

Many developers will read this book and see that a number of Web XP practices are not very far off from some of the things they are doing already. When we first started getting into XP, our coach Chet Hennrickson told us that we were already doing XP in our graphical design process. From there we tried a practice here and there before making the full commitment to go XP. We would urge anyone considering Extreme Programming for their Web projects to do the same.

Start with how you engage with customers. If you are in a fixed-price, fixed-scope arrangement, you will have to fake it for a while. All your stories will be predefined but you will be able to let your customer decide in which order they are done. Call it the "Planning Game Lite." Your customer will welcome getting working code in regular iterative releases and will like getting to set priorities.

The goal here is for them to learn about the benefits of XP and to feel like part of the team. If you can build up trust, then perhaps your next phase of development can be under an iterative work-effort driven contact instead of fixed price and/or fixed scope.

Next you will want to experiment with paired development and writing your first unit test. Do these at the same time to get the team working together and sharing what is learned as all of you stumble through your first few tests.

Get help. Find a coach who has experience in XP to help guide the way; this person can be someone who works onsite with the team or just someone who the team can email with questions. Failing a warm body, this "coach" could be one of the online XP communities or a local XP users group; most major cities have an XP meeting every month.

Finally, change the way you build Web sites. If you take only one thing away from this book, let it be to say goodbye to HTML and start following the XML patterns we have defined here. In our experience, this has made the most difference.

References

Publications

Averby, Christine Spivey, and Paul Sonderegger, with Harley Manning, Julie Meriger, Aaron Hardisty, and Sadaf Roshon, *eCommerce Integrators Exposed*. Forrester Research, June 2000.

Beck, Kent. *Extreme Programming Explained: Embrace Change*. Addison-Wesley, 2000.

Wilkinson, Nancy M. *Using CRC Cards: An Informal Approach to Object-Oriented Development*. SIGS Books and Multimedia, 1995.

Web Sites

http://axkit.org
http://c2.com/cgi/wiki?ExtremeProgrammingCorePractices
http://msdn.microsoft.com
http://tidy.sourceforge.net/
http://www.servletsuite.com/servlets/xmlflt.htm
http://www.w3.org/TR/xhtml1/
http://xml.apache.org/cocoon
http://xsltunit.org

Further Reading

Here are some of the books that helped us along the way and that still teach us new ways of looking at projects.

For Everyone

The Mythical Man-Month, Essays on Software Engineering, Anniversary Edition, by Frederick P. Brooks, Addison-Wesley, 1995.

> Some of the projects described in this book are so large and complex that we might wonder what the modern developer has to complain about. We quickly see that today's project management issues are the same as they ever were.

Information Architecture for the World Wide Web, by Louis Rosenfeld and Peter Morville, O'Reilly & Associates, 1998.

> Navigation is the single largest determinant of a site's success or failure. The best content is worthless if it is hidden away from the user. This book is about design patterns for Web sites and will serve as a daily companion for the Web professional.

Web Content Management: A Collaborative Approach, by Russell Nakano, Addison-Wesley, 2002.

> Working together to gather Web site content and then maintain it is a major theme in Web development. This practical guide dovetails with the XP approach and its strategies for filling out the content aspects of a mature Web release plan.

Agile Software Development with SCRUM, by Ken Schwaber, Mike Beedle, and Robert C. Martin, Prentice Hall, 2002.

> XP is the first of a group of "agile" development practices. SCRUM is new to us, but it deals with the same themes as XP and so deserves a look.

For Strategists

The 11 Immutable Laws of Internet Branding, by Al Ries and Laura Ries, HarperBusiness, 2000.

> Short and easy to read, this book is a slap in the face to traditional wisdom about what the Internet means to companies. Every step of the XP process is aimed at delivering business value. No strategist should tell a client what to do with her site without pondering this book for a while.

For Project Managers

Software Project Survival Guide, by Steve C. McConnell, Microsoft Press, 1998.

> Like *The Mythical Man-Month,* this book is a primer on the nature of software projects, many of which have been saved by its advice. New project managers will avoid years of tears by taking a hard look at the discussion of risks and how to mitigate them.

For Developers

Refactoring: Improving the Design of Existing Code, by Martin Fowler with Kent Beck, John Brant, William Opdyke, and Don Roberts, Addison-Wesley, 1999.

> How can code get better, not worse, over time? This seminal book is the first step to manageable systems and to the fulfillment of the quality promise in XP.

Code Complete: A Practical Handbook of Software Construction, by Steve C. McConnell, Microsoft Press, 1993.

> Refactoring and unit tests are a big part of XP, but they don't replace the art of writing good code. This book is a standard in the community of developers who are serious about their craft.

Using CRC Cards: An Informal Approach to Object-Oriented Development, by Nancy M. Wilkinson, SIGS Books and Multimedia, 1995.

> CRC card sessions are at the heart of developing architectures as a team. What if no one on the team has done one before? Wilkinson's book gives in-depth step-by-step instructions.

Enterprise Application Integration, by David S. Linthicum, Addison-Wesley, 2000.

> Web projects are constantly faced with exposing legacy systems to the Internet. How do big systems work together? This book clearly lays out various integration strategies with clear pros and cons for each.

UML Distilled: A Brief Guide to the Standard Object Modeling Language, Second Edition, by Martin Fowler and Kendall Scott, Addison-Wesley, 2000.

> A good primer and desk reference for UML, this book covers a lot of ground in an approachable manner.

Building Web Applications with UML, Second Edition, by Jim Conallen, Addison-Wesley, 2003.

> This book was a major inspiration for adapting XP to Web projects. UML is a useful, simple, and flexible documenting tool to describe software. But it is not so good for describing how software intertwines with Web pages. Conallen has bent UML just enough to allow difficult structures like frames and content to fit into documents that can be shared with programmers, designers, and customers. XP is document light, not document free. We highly recommend Conallen's notation when it comes time to crack open Visio.

Learning XML, by Erik T. Ray, O'Reilly & Associates, 2001.

> This book is a good starting place for developers new to XML.

Essential XML Quick Reference: A Programmer's Reference to XML, XPath, XSLT, XML Schema, SOAP, and More, by Aaron Skonnard and Martin Gudgin, Addison-Wesley, 2002.

> An excellent reference guide for experienced XML developers.

For the Designer

User-Centered Web Design, by John Cato, Addison-Wesley, 2001.

> "Never forget who the audience is" is the refrain in this very grounded approach to how people use Web sites and systems.

Designing Web Usability: The Practice of Simplicity, by Jakob Nielsen, New Riders Publishing, 2000.

> Very XP. Nielsen's straightforward and lightweight suggestions help sites communicate with their audience without gimmicks or fanfare.

Index

DTDs, 91
    standardization of, 96
Dummy XML, 101–102

E

Equation-based estimates, 14–15
Estimates
    parameters of, 15–17
    pitfalls of, 14–15
    problems of, 21–22, 117
    for projects. *See* Project estimation
    stories in, 64, 66
    of velocity, 127–128
    XML in 95–109
    XP-based, 17–18
Estimation, and planning, 65–66
Extensible HTML. *See* XHTML
Extensible Markup Language.
        See XML
Experience-based estimates, 15
Extreme Programming. *See* XP

F

Fixed-price quotes, 15, 17
Formatting, separated from
        content, 97–98
Fowler, Martin, 132
Function points, 35
Functionality, server-side, 149

G

Graphic design
    customer input into, 76
    iterations for, 76–82
    sample designs, 79–81
    specs for, 81
Graphic designer
    paired with interface program-
        mer, 48

    paired with tester, 49
    in Web XP project, 44
Greeking, 102

H

Hennrickson, Chet, 152
HTML, 86
    abandoning, 153
    characteristics of Web pages in,
        89–90
    disadvantages of, 85, 87–88
HTTPUnit, 88, 148

I

Image tags, 110
Integration, continuous. *See* Con-
    tinuous integration
Interface programmer
    paired with graphic
        designer, 48
    in Web XP project, 43–44
Interoperability, maintaining, 96
ISAPI filter, 112
Iteration, 61
    and graphic design, 76–82
    guidelines for, 118
    ideal length of, 119, 122
    and matching tasks, 82
    planning and estimating, 65–66,
        120
    strategy session for, 63–65,
        119–120
Iteration 1
    function of, 67–68
    importance of, 67
    stories for, 68
Iteration 2
    function of, 69
    stories for, 70

The XP Series

Kent Beck, Series Advisor

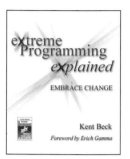

The XP manifesto

0201616416

Planning projects with XP

0201710919

Insights and practical wisdom from leaders in the XP community

0201770059

Get XP up and running in your organization

0201708426

Best XP practices

0201710404

Is XP right for your organization?

0201844575

Learn from the chronicle of an XP project

0201709376

Best XP practices for developers

0201733978

Master the intricacies of XP testing

0321113551

Practical advice from experienced practitioners on how to get started with XP

0201616408

Apply XP to web projects

0201794276